IMAGES OF ENGLAND

# THE LOST ALLEYS OF
# TEWKESBURY

IMAGES OF ENGLAND

# THE LOST ALLEYS OF
# TEWKESBURY

CLIFF BURD

TEMPUS

*Frontispiece:* Tolsey Lane, leading towards the High Street and a fishmonger's shop. Tolsey comes from the old word for the town hall, which was located close to this lane.

First published 2004

Tempus Publishing Limited
The Mill, Brimscombe Port,
Stroud, Gloucestershire, GL5 2QG

British Library Cataloguing in Publication Data.
A catalogue record for this book is available from the British Library.

ISBN 0 7524 3189 7

Typesetting and origination by Tempus Publishing Limited
Printed in Great Britain by Midway Colour Print, Wiltshire

# Contents

# Acknowledgements

I WOULD LIKE TO THANK all those people who have helped to compile and layout this book, especially my son Nick for his computer expertise, and my wife, Pat, for her encouragement and forbearance, and to John Dixon for reading and correcting the text, and providing information gathered during his own research. I wish to thank all those people with local knowledge who have passed on stories and information about the town and the people living here. If there are any errors in this book, I apologise, and hope that readers will feel happy to inform me.

Aerial view of the town showing the Abbey with playing fields in the background, in around 1930.

# Introduction

THE ALLEYS AND COURTS OF Tewkesbury have proved to be a fascinating subject for research – fascinating but extremely frustrating. For the past two years or so, a series of talks about the existing alleys has proved to be of great interest, not only to the people living in the town, but to groups in Cheltenham, Gloucester and most of the villages in the surrounding district.

In his *History of Tewkesbury*, James Bennett lists a number of these thoroughfares, as required by the town council, in the mid-nineteenth century. John Rogers, in his *Short History of the old Alleys Courts and Lanes of the Borough* which was published by Collections of Barton Street, and written at around the turn of the twentieth century, and more recently, *Theot Guppy and Wulf* by Brian Linnell, have also given us the results of their research. These insights into a unique feature of the town, have led me to try to give a definitive listing of all the alleys and courts that have disappeared.

Having lived for more than a hundred years, John Rogers was able to give us information based on his personal knowledge and experience of the people living in the town. Brian Linnel obviously did an enormous amount of research, giving us dates, locations and alternative names for a large number of alleys and courts.

All researchers feel the frustration of information and detail being just out of reach, entirely because of their pursuit of the information held in the records or in the memories of older generations. If only Rogers had identified some of the locations by street numbers, and if the early census returns had only carried a little more information regarding relationships or occupations, then life would be much simpler for the researchers!

Someone said that the problems associated with identifying all the pubs, their sites and their owners were very frustrating. This I believe, but would suggest that trying to weave a path through the changes of names and locations of these thoroughfares creates some problems that are almost insurmountable. The re-numbering of the streets only serves to

*Opposite:* Old Baptist Church court, c.1900. The chapel dates from 1623 and was one of the earliest in the country. The chapel on the left was at this time converted into two cottages.

St Marys Lane, c.1950. The garage was a timber-framed property, which should have been saved but was demolished, together with the old chemical works behind it, to make access for the rear of The Royal Hop Pole.

compound the problems. While on the subject of numbering, readers should note that there was a change in the numbering of the streets in 1871 – a change designed to catch out the unwary researcher. The dates used here are post-1871.

The naming of these passageways is of great importance to the history of the town. Those that carry the name of a pub are, of course, self-explanatory and, as in the case of The Red Lion and The Unicorn, have changed when the name of the pub changed. Most of the remainder are family names, where the owner of the property facing onto the street would give the name to the alley, for example, Pullocks Alley changing to Evans Alley. Sometimes the name came from the owner of the property in the alley, and when these families moved, the name of the alley changed, and the new owner identified the place. There are exceptions: Fish Alley is one example where perhaps the name reflected the occupation, as it does in Nailers Alley and Nailers Square. There are instances where an alley has become a court over a period of time, e.g. Ancills Court was originally an alley running through to Swilgate Road. Some of the earlier changes probably came about with one or more of the residents deciding to stop at one end of the alley. Later, when the local authorities were more vigilant, two or more members of the council would be nominated to investigate the usage by the general public and recommend to the council if a Closure Order was a sensible move. However, some such as Summers Court, have never been alleys.

The names of the alleys, the people who lived, worked, and eventually died there, are the story of the town itself. They reflect the growth of the town, its industry, its fortunes and misfortunes, and, I believe, the character of the town.

The database held on computer in the library has been an enormous boon to those wishing to research the town or their own family history, and it is from here that a good deal of the information has been obtained.

Searching through this data gives one an insight into the lives of the people living here over the past two centuries, but discipline in any research of this kind is difficult, and it is easy to get sidetracked. The dreadful conditions are highlighted alongside the humorous, as in the case of one George Davis, of Myrtle Court, who in 1884 was charged by the police, with an assault on his wife, Harriett[1]. He was a naval pensioner with only one arm and one leg! One cannot help but wonder how he managed it. On 26 August 1832, Thomas Painter – a stocking maker aged thirty-four and living in Boulters Court, died of cholera[2]. Within half an hour, his wife had also died of the same disease. Was there a family, and if so, what happened to them?

I have tried to verify the details in the following pages by searching more than one source, wherever this has been possible. However, there are some names that have perhaps only had one mention, for instance, Bubbs Alley, noted by Norah Day in her book, *They Were Born in Tewkesbury*. This alley appears to have been in Church Street and may be Lilleys Alley, but this is only conjecture. Chambers Court is mentioned by Linnell as being unlocated, but a report in the *Tewkesbury Register* dated 26 November 1883, records that George Alexander Russell of Chambers Court had died, aged twenty-two. Consequently, such areas will be recorded with what little information has come to light.

As the town developed and the frontages of the main streets were built upon, it was inevitable that any further housing would be built at right angles to the main streets.

Ancills Alley, which is now Ancills Court, c.1970. The garage on the right was part of an old slaughterhouse, while next to it is a manure pit. The alley runs from Church Street, alongside the Berkley Arms, down to Swilgate Road.

A view of Church Street from a window in a building in Barton Street. The street has been washed down, which is a practice sadly missing today. Note the workman on the left, who is probably painting the Plough Inn sign.

Limitations on the land available for building was due to the rivers and brooks surrounding the town, and the low-lying land, which was liable to flooding.

The movement of people from the truly rural areas into the towns, and the rising birth rate, created a demand for cheaper rented accommodation. It was not only sought after in Tewkesbury, but also across most of the towns and cities in the country. However, the effect on Tewkesbury was greater because of its location.

John Rogers tells us that some of the housing in the alleys were built 'in the old Tewkesbury style', by which he would have meant timber framed. Alas – most of what remained at the time of his report has now disappeared, being swept away in the name of development. A large number however, were brick-built terraced cottages, of two and three storeys, with a doorway leading straight into the alley, and a window on each floor.

The size of the cottages depended on the frontage property; if this was a full 'burgage', then the tenements would be bigger, offering a space for a garden or a pigsty, which were necessary for feeding the family.

In some cases, the alley would open out into a square, as in Huntleys Court on Barton Street. Later a water pump may have been added, or much later, even a tap, which was such luxury! This would also provide a drying area for the family washing and a general communal space. Where there was a generous landlord, a well may have been sunk to provide water for a number of properties, but this was unusual in an alley. In some cases a water butt to catch rainwater would have been used, but in many areas of the town, water would have been obtained from the rivers in buckets.

The *Tewkesbury Register* of 1860 made an issue of the problems of sanitation, or the lack of it. The editor was particularly severe on the fact that there was no sewage system. Swilgate Brook, into which a good proportion of the towns sewage flowed, was like a cesspit, and it was said that 'the stench is almost unbearable'. The main drains, which were built in 1824, took surface water from the three main roads, with five outlets into the Mill Avon and three into Swilgate Brook[3]. With part of the population taking water from these sources for daily consumption, there was obviously a need to channel this waste further downstream, to Lower Lode Lane for example.

The Council set about tackling the problem in a piecemeal fashion, which meant that while Swilgate Brook was being cleared, the Mill Avon gradually got worse. If the Abbey Mill was not in operation for a while, then the water did not flow and the debris accumulated. Therefore, it is small wonder that cholera and typhoid ran through the town at regular intervals when we remember that water for domestic use was taken from these waterways.

When cholera did strike the town, it invariably started in one of the alleys and then spread quickly through the town, claiming lives indiscriminately. Part of the remedy at the time, was to burn the bedclothes and then limewash the walls, in the belief that lime was a deterrent or a cure. In the 1849 outbreak, the Council set aside a house in Oldbury Road to try to isolate the disease. This was a wise move, given the level of ignorance about these diseases. At this time, it was considered adequate for there to be one privy per alley, despite the fact that some, such as Double Alley, had almost one hundred inhabitants

Traditionally, it became the practice to limewash the alley walls and apply tar to the bottom foot of the walls. The older residents will tell that the limewash formula included 'sheep dung', which was perhaps to improve its stickiness! (This practice of limewashing has not been kept up unfortunately, but at the time of writing, there is a move afoot to reintroduce whitewashing on a limited number of alleys each year.)

Although the aim had been to have a hand water pump in every alley, this was not really achieved, and where there was a pump it didn't always work. In his inquiry in 1849[4], Mr Rammell found that the pump in Double Alley had not worked for three years, while the one in Townsends Alley had been inoperable for seven years! Nineteen of the alleys were without any sanitary provisions whatsoever.

Piped water eventually came to the town in around 1870[5], but only because Cheltenham was looking to obtain a supply from the river, for its growing population, and wanted to pipe it through the streets of Tewkesbury. The foundations of the waterworks at the Mythe were laid in 1869, accompanied by a procession and brass bands.

There were some attempts at keeping the town clean, with the council making regulations at intervals. In the seventeenth century, one such regulation declared that butchers and fishmongers were not to leave rubbish in the streets, pigs and sows were not to wander in the streets, and dead dogs were not to be ignored! Householders and shopkeepers were responsible for cleaning and maintaining the pavement in front of their property and for cleaning the gutters[6]. In 1786, an Act was obtained for 'paving lighting cleaning and

Tewkesbury Abbey from the air, 1925.

repairing the streets, lanes, ways, passages and places of the town'.[7] Prior to this, a deep and muddy gutter had run down the centre of the main streets, with lesser ones from the several lanes and alleys uniting with them.

At this time, the streets were deemed so dangerous that poor persons would station themselves at the main entrances to the town, and for a small charge would escort the horses of travellers through the town[8].

In the following text, for the sake of clarity and to avoid any confusion, the names of the alleys have been given without any apostrophes, for example, Turner's Alley is given as it is spoken – Turners Alley.

1   *Tewkesbury Register*
2   Cholera Report
3   Anthea Jones
4   Report, Rammell
5   Anthea Jones
6   Tewk. Reg
7   Gloucestershire Records Office
8   Anthea Jones

# CHAPTER ONE

# List of Streets

THE FOLLOWING IS A LIST OF alley and court names which have been found.

| | ALTERNATIVE NAMES | LOCATION |
|---|---|---|
| **MILL STREET** | | |
| Wakeleys Court | | Entrance from Mill Bank |
| Mill Court | | Entrance from Mill Street |
| | | |
| **CHURCH STREET** | | |
| Aurora Passage | Buckles Court | |
| | Whiteheads Court | No.39–40 |
| Bagalleys Alley | | Not located |
| Bank Alley | Reads Alley | |
| | Pittways Alley | No.99–100 |
| Boulters Alley | Butchers Alley | No.88–89 |
| Bubbs Alley | Lilley's Alley | No.9–10 |
| Buckles Alley | Aurora | |
| | Whiteheads | No.39–40 |
| Butchers Alley | Boulters Alley | |
| | Punch Bowl? | No.88–89 |
| Bull Passage | | No.96–97 |
| Finches Alley | Woodwards Alley | No.58–59 |
| Freemans Court | Turners Court | No.83–84 |
| Gibbs Court | | No.49–50 |
| Harris Alley | Mathews Alley | No.4–5 |
| Insalls Alley | | No.8–9 |
| Insalls Court | Smiths Court | No.73–74 |

| | ALTERNATIVE NAMES | LOCATION |
|---|---|---|
| Laights Court | | No.85–86 |
| Lewis Court | | Not located |
| Longs Alley | | Not located |
| Mathews Alley | Harris Alley | No.4–5 |
| Mayalls Court | | No.74–75 |
| Nicholls Alley | | No.18–19 |
| Packers Court | | No.10–11 |
| Pittways Alley | Reads Alley | |
| | Bank Alley | No.99–100 |
| Punch Bowl Alley | Boulters | |
| | Butchers | No.89–90 |
| Quart Pot Alley | | No.5–6 |
| Reads Alley | Bank Alley | |
| | Pittways Alley | No.99–100 |
| Savings Bank Alley | | No.5–6 |
| Walkers Alley | Walkers Lane | No.68–69 |
| Whiteheads Alley | Buckles, Aurora | No.39–40 |
| Woodwards Alley | Finches | No.58–59 |
| | | |
| **HIGH STREET** | | |
| Barrel Passage | Kedwards Court | No.33–34 |
| Bedford Court | | No.82–83 |
| Bishop's Court | | No.82–82 |

| | ALTERNATIVE NAMES | LOCATION | | ALTERNATIVE NAMES | LOCATION |
|---|---|---|---|---|---|
| Bronds Court | Broads Court | No.90–91 | Redells Alley | | No.6–7 |
| Castle Alley | Double, Harris, | | Red Lion Alley | Unicorn Alley | No.84–85 |
| | Oldbury Walk | No.87–88. | Scotts Alley | Clothiers Alley | No.122–123 |
| Clothiers Alley | Scotts Alley | No.122–123 | Sparkes Alley | George Passage | |
| Codringtons Alley | | No.119–120 | | Jeynes Alley | No.54–55 |
| Collins Alley | | Not located | Sperrys Alley | Walls Court | No.129–130 |
| Culls Alley | | No.139–140 | Spilburys Alley | | No.17–18 |
| Dixons Alley | Machine Court | No.34–35 | Strawfords Court | Glovers, Townsends | |
| Dobbins Alley | Clarkes Alley | | | and Mansells | No.88–89 |
| | Wilkinsons Alley | No.49–50 | Steels Court | | No.84–85 |
| Double Alley | Castles, Harris | | Summers Alley | | No.76–77 |
| | Oldbury Walk | No.87–88 | Strawfords Alley | | Not located |
| Garratts Alley | | No.81–82 | Sun Alley | Old Sun Street | |
| George Passage | Jeynes Alley, | | Taylors Alley | Wilkes Alley | No.23–24 |
| | Sparkes Alley | No.54–55 | Townsends Alley | Mansells, Glovers | No.88–89 |
| Glovers Alley | Mansells Alley | | Unicorn Alley | Red Lion Alley | No.84–85 |
| | Townsends | No.88–89 | Wadleys Alley | Predys Alley | Not located |
| Gotheridges Alley | | Not located | Waldrons Court | Broads Court | No.90–91 |
| Harris Alley | Double Alley | | Wheatsheaf Passage | | No.131–132 |
| | Castles | | Wilkinsons Alley | Clarkes Alley | |
| | Oldbury Walk | No.87–88 | | Dobbins Alley | No.49–50 |
| Haywards Alley | Malverns Alley | No.125–126 | | | |
| Heaths Alley | | No.130–131 | **BARTON STREET** | | |
| Hodges Alley | Eagles Alley | No.110–111 | Andrews Court | | No.11–12 |
| Jeynes Alley | George Passage | | Archers | | No.77–78 |
| | Sparkes Alley | No.54–55 | Batchelors Court | | Not located |
| Justins Alley | | No.16–17 | Baughtons | | Not located |
| Johnsons Alley | | Not located | Bells Alley | Fish Alley, | |
| Kedwards Alley | Barrell Passage | No.33–34 | | Joyces Alley | No.69–70 |
| Lanes Alley | | No.135–136 | Boulters Alley | | No.88a–89 |
| Malverns Alley | Haywards Alley | No.125–126 | Burrows Court | | No.63–64 |
| Mansells Court | Glovers Alley | | Collins Court | Longs Alley | No.26–27 |
| | Townsends Alley | No.88–89 | Costnetts Alley | Woods Court | No.35–36 |
| Mayalls Court | | No.89–90 | Crooked Alley | Alexander Court | No.12–13 |
| Oddfellows Passage | | No.109 | Evans Alley | Pullocks Alley | No.67–68 |
| Oldbury Walk | Double Alley | | Finchers Alley | | No.57–58 |
| | Castles, Harris | No.87–88 | Freemans Court | | No.54–55 |
| Predys Alley | Wadleys Alley | Not located | Gannaways Court | | Not located |
| Roberts Court | | No.112–113 | Greens Alley | Masons Court | No.82–83 |

|  | ALTERNATIVE NAMES | LOCATION |
|---|---|---|
| Harewoods Alley | Charlewoods Alley | No.24–25 |
| Huntleys Court |  | No.19–20 |
| Joyces Alley | Fish Alley |  |
|  | Bells Alley | No.69–70 |
| Longs Alley | Collins Court | No.26–27 |
| Millards Court |  | No.6–7 |
| Myrtle Court |  | Off Hughes Alley |
| Morris Alley |  | In the area of Nelson Street |
| Nailors Alley |  | No.21–22 |
| Nelsons Alley |  | No.20–21 |
| Parkers Court |  | No.56–57 |
| Peacheys Court |  | No.71–72 |
| Pullocks Alley | Evans Alley | No.67–6 |
| Thomas Alley |  | No.22–23 |
| Tysoes Passage |  | No.5–7 |
| Whites Court |  | No.49 |
| Whiteheads Court |  | No.61–62 |
| Workhouse Alley | Hughes Alley | No.69–70 |

## OLDBURY ROAD

| Alexander Place | Corner of Nelson Street and Oldbury Road |
|---|---|
| Bleach Yard | Between Walls Court and Old Post Office Alley |
| Dallingers Court | Not located |
| Dobbins Court | Between Tracy Row and Hollams Road |
| Merretts Court | Opposite East Street, Rear of High Street |
| School Court | Trinity School area. |
| Wellington Place | Not located |

## BACK OF AVON

### (was Quay Street North and Quay street South)

| Birds Court | Corner of Smith's Lane and Back of Avon |
|---|---|
| Catherines Court | Off Tolsey Lane, area demolished. |
| Nailors Square | Tolsey Lane? |
| Rices Court | Tolsey Lane? |
| Sweets Court | Corner of Smith's Lane and Back of Avon |

## EAST STREET

| Clays Court | Name taken from Clays Buildings |
|---|---|
| Wrights Court | At the rear of 39 Barton Street |

## UNLOCATED ALLEYS

| Blizards Court | Perhaps near the site of Blizzard and Colemans, or Church Street where the family lived. However, a report in the *Tewkesbury Register* of April 1884, records that the house in the High Street fronting Bishops Alley, was occupied by Edward Blizzard, which is another possibility. |
|---|---|
| Chambers Court | Not yet located |
| Reeves Alley or Court | The Reeves sisters had a shop at The Cross, but I believe that the court name refers to an earlier site. |
| Johnsons Alley | Not yet located |
| Lewis Court | Not yet located |

Lilleys Alley, Church Street.

The following chapters give the names and alternatives, and where it has been possible to ascertain them, the street numbers of the alleys.

Let the text take you on a tour of the town, alley by alley, beginning at Mill Street. Then go along the north side of Church Street North to The Cross, then up the west side of the High Street and down the east side, back to The Cross. Next, to the north side of Barton Street and then back along the opposite side to The Cross. Along the south side as far as The Abbey. The Oldbury Road is then followed by Tolsey Lane and the Back of Avon, and finally to East Street.

A little imagination in trying to visualise the people working in these alleys, in cramped, and by today's standards, sordid conditions, may help the reader understand what life was like in the town.

# CHAPTER TWO

# Mill Street

## Mill Court

According to the map of 1883, the access appears to be covered leading off Mill Street, and there are three properties here. In the census of 1851, John Roberts was in residence and at age fifty he was working as a tanner, perhaps at the tannery in St Marys Lane. He and his wife had three children: Harriett, aged seventeen and a stocking-maker, John aged fifteen and a miller, and Emma aged nine. Thomas Hooper is a stocking-maker living here, with his wife and eldest son doing the same job.

Millbank.

*Left:* Mill Street, c.1950, from the Old Mill end of the street. The old building on the right has been used for many things, including a brewery and an art gallery. This part of town would originally have been inside the old abbey walls.

*Below left:* Mill Bank looking towards the Borough Mill, showing the hand pump and water trough. Note the hay rick on the Ham Field, c.1950.

*Below:* Wakeleys Court, leading from Mill Bank

## Wakeleys Court

Located at the end of Mill Bank, this was once a thoroughfare to Church Street. The Feoffee Charity Trust owned the property in the court. I have been unable to find any record of the name, but would reasonably assume it to be a family name.

CHAPTER THREE
# Church Street North

### Finches Alley
Not to be confused with Finchers Alley, which was located in Barton Street, this one was also known as Woodwards Alley and was situated at Nos 58-59 Church Street.

### Walkers Alley
The area where this alley would have been has long been built over. It would have run from Church Street through to St Marys Lane at Nos 68-69 Church Street. The name would have derived from Walkers Lane in the eighteenth century. A hotel now sits on the site.

### Insalls Court
John Insall was a cordwainer (boot and shoe maker), living at what we now know as Smiths Court, at No. 72 Church Street. It is the only alley that still retains the old hand water pump which was originally used by the residents, but is long since out of use.

### Mayalls Court
This alley was located at Nos 74-75 Church Street, and refers to the Mayall family. Just two doors further along from the previous court, it is still possible to see a section of the old alley by entering Smiths Court. The alley is to the right hand side of the old hand-water pump. In 1861, there were four families living here, made up of just ten people. Joshua Griffin, aged twenty-six, is listed as a photographer and painter and he had a wife and a daughter.

### Freemans Court
This is the court now known as Turners Court at Nos 83-84, and as such has not disappeared. Again, there is another court of this name in Barton Street, which is recorded later.

*Left:* Mayalls Court, which is now closed off but is still visible from Smiths Court.

*Below:* Boulters or Punch Bowl Alley. This is the entrance from Church Street.

## Boulters Alley

Also known as Butchers Alley, it was situated at Nos 88-89 Church Street where Thomas Boulter worked as a butcher in around 1813. The census of 1841 indicates that only two families were living here. Thomas Newman was a thirty-eight-year-old blacksmith with four children aged seven to thirteen years, but there is no record of a wife. The other family consists of James Coombes, a twenty-nine-year-old framework knitter, his wife Mary and a daughter aged four.

## Punch Bowl Alley

Named after a public house in Church Street, this name came to light late in research, when it was noted in documents held at the Records Office in Gloucester. The record states 'the said alley or passage belonging to the said messuage lately called the Punch Bowl leading from St Mary's Lane', and is dated 1809. In 1803, the pub was called the Eight Bells, and was formerly The Royal Oak, but the name of the alley does not seem to have changed with the name of the pub. Details in these documents indicate that the alley was located near or at, Nos 89-90 Church Street, which would make this an alternative name for Boulters Alley.

At the rear of the building it is still possible to see the remains of the blue-brick alley floor leading down the garden.

## Bull Passage

This is the entrance of Nos 96–97 Church Street, where Edward Edgell lived. He was the grandfather of Beatrice Edgell – the renowned psychologist who attended Tewkesbury High School. Two families were living in the alley, and both the husbands were journeyman tanners, at a part of the tanning industry located in the St Marys Lane area. In the 1868 poll, there was only one voter registered: Silas Vine, who was a labourer. This was also known as Bull Court and Bull Alley, and in 1868, the Poll List shows Silas Vine, a farm labourer, living here and voting for Price, the Liberal candidate. This was unusual as only skilled working class men had a vote. Silas was still here in 1871, with his wife and daughter. William Edwards also lived in the court. He was a fifty-four-year-old farm labourer, with a wife aged thirty-four and three sons.

## Bank Alley

This alley sits between the Hat Shop and a fast food shop at Nos 99–100 Church Street. The name comes from Hartlands Bank, which was in business from the mid-nineteenth century until the 1920s. This is an old alley, which had thirteen cottages all on the north side. The alley is now closed off, and has a carved panel over the heavy doorway, with the initials R.R.

Bull Passage, located next door to The Royal Hop Pole.

and a date of 1664 inscribed on it. Having had the opportunity to view the property recently, (July 2002), it was found possible to see an old entrance into the front of the ground floor from the alley, where it had been bricked up. It is where another entrance had replaced it at a much later date, which is also now bricked up.

In the 1841 census there were forty people living in the alley, and two of the houses were empty. The population fluctuated, and by 1851 there were eight families here and a total of twenty-seven residents. Four of the families: Pitts, Webb, Hall and Rodgers were there from the previous census. By 1881 there were only two families recorded: the Parsons and the Prossers, which were each made up of five people. There was no indication in the census of what was happening to the other properties. However, ten years later, nine of the cottages were occupied with thirty people in residence.

The cholera epidemic of 1832 took washerwoman Ann Webb, who was aged fifty-two, on 20 August. In the 1849 outbreak two people died: labourer John Symons, aged fifty-two, and a boy aged four, called Thomas Pitts, who was buried at the workhouse. All of these were from Bank Alley.

The poll book of 1868 shows that only five people from Bank Alley were registered to vote: James Webster – a labourer, James Godsall – a nailer, Richard Nicholls – a labourer living at No. 8 and James Parsons and James Wise, who were both labourers.

*Left:* The inside of Bank Alley, looking toward Church Street.

*Opposite:* Bank Alley, with the entrance to the left of the the Hat Shop. This is now closed and the cottages have been demolished.

The rear of the Hat Shop,
Bank Alley in Church Street.

A report in the *Tewkesbury Register*, dated March 1895, stated that 'One in eight cottages shared water', and in the same newspaper, in January 1920, it was reported that the owners of nine cottages in Bank Alley were ordered to 'provide sufficient water closets for these cottages'.

The state of these alley houses can be measured by the fact that in February 1921, five of them were sold to T. Mellor, for the sum of £33.

In 1924, the rent for a cottage in Bank Alley was 1s 7d, per week.

## Pittways Alley

This was also known as Reads Alley and Bank Alley, and was situated at Nos 99–100 Church Street.

# CHAPTER FOUR

# High Street

### Redells Alley

The site of a printers and stationers shop situated at No. 6 High Street, next to the Nodding Gables. An early photograph of Redells shop indicates that the entrance was probably at the right hand side of the shop, at what is now the entrance to a ladies hairdresser.

### Justins Alley

There was only one family in residence that was recorded in the census of 1861, and located at Nos 16-17 High Street: William Prewin aged twenty-eight, and employed as a Cordwainer, and his wife Louisa, aged thirty-two, a shoe binder. No other information has come to light for this alley.

### Spilburys Alley

This old alley which is long gone, was named after a local surgeon who lived in the High Street. The alley would have been located between Nos 17-18 High Street. It was extinguished in the first decade of the nineteenth century.

### Taylors Alley

This was an earlier name for Wilkes Alley, which is the next one along the High Street. It is obviously a family name, but I can find no other record.

### Kedwards Alley

This is the alley which is now known as Barrel Passage at Nos 33-34 High Street. John Kedward was a butcher operating from the front shop in around 1830. There were cottages going down to the Mill Avon until around 1965. The alley was diverted to accommodate the building of Hanover Court flats in 1970. The *Tewkesbury Register* of 20 September 1873, reported that one of the houses in Kedwards Alley had thirty people sleeping in the loft! One would assume that this would have been a lodging house.

## Barrel Passage

The name comes from the Barrel Pub, which was at No. 34 High Street – the site now filled by the Somerfield supermarket. Earlier it was known as Kedwards Alley, after John Kedward, who was a butcher owning a shop there.

John Rogers states that this was known as Machine Court in about 1848, and that the houses in the alley were owned by Fowler & Co. of Stratford-upon-Avon. I have not been able to verify this as Machine Court, and Linnel does not have this record.

*Left:* The site of Redells Alley, in the High Street.

*Below:* The upper part of the High Street, close to the Sabrina Cinema. Shakespeare's shop front survives, but his business has been closed for some time. Here, seven of the alleys and courts were demolished in the restructuring of the High Street.

*Opposite:* The George Passage, which is also Jeynes Alley in around 1920. The entrance is to the left of the picture.

A valuation dated 1910, shows that the cottages were at that time owned by Flowers Brewery, as was the pub. A rent of 2s 3d, per week was charged for a cottage. It would have two bedrooms and a ground floor living room, while outside there would be the usual shared WC and a washhouse. At this time there were two tenants quoted, George Sharp and William Titcombe.

## Dixons Court

This was the family name given to the existing Machine Court.

## Dobbins Alley

This was the earlier name given to Clarkes Alley at Nos 49-50 High Street, and is still remaining. It was also known as Wilkinsons Alley. The name may well have come from Dobbins Row, as the owner had a business in the High Street.

## Wilkinsons Alley

An alley that has been known as Dobbins Alley, and is still with us, but now called Clarkes Alley.

## George Passage

This passage took its name from the public house at Nos 54-55 High Street, and had two other names. It was called Jeynes Alley in 1841 and before this in around 1808, it went under the name of Sparkes Alley.

In 1841, Jeynes Alley had twenty-two residents living in six cottages. Aaron Boswell, who was aged forty-five, is defined as a Canal Agent, living here with his wife. Perhaps this was a temporary lodging, and Aaron was working locally on the river, or possibly the locks, following his profession.

By 1851 there were only two cottages occupied. Mr Boswell has gone, of course. Mary Mills was forty-nine years old and is called a 'Maltsters Wife'. She is named as the head of the house in the census, so her husband is away from home at this time. She has five children, and the eldest, Samuel, is a cordwainer.

## Jeynes Alley

An alternative name for George Passage. Jeynes is an old Tewkesbury family name, active in business in the nineteenth century.

## Sparkes Alley

Another name for George Passage and Jeynes Alley.

## Garretts Alley

This alley was sited at Nos 81–82 High Street, and named after John Garrett. Linnel states that it was closed off in around 1900, and that the area was demolished 1932, but it is shown on the 1883 map.

## Bedford Court

This court was originally named Marshalls Alley, after the owner of the greengrocers shop kept by Mr Marshall. Mr Bedford was a painter by trade, and he took the front house after Mr Marshall left in the early part of the nineteenth century. According to John Rogers, he also owned some of the cottages in the alley. The upper part of the alley, which leads on to the Red Lion Alley, was later closed off. The cottages were typical of all the alleys: one room on the first and second floors, a kitchen on the ground floor and a shared washhouse and WC, (no flush). The rent paid by Thomas Green was 1s 3d, and by Mr F. Allen 2s 1d, per week.

## Bishops Court

This was originally called an alley, and located at Nos 82–83 High Street. It was part of the town which fell prey to the bulldozers in 1965. *Pigots Directory* of 1830, shows Elizabeth Bishop living on the front of the High Street. According to Linnell, Mr Bishop was a butcher with his business here on the left side of the alley. Further down the alley he had his slaughterhouse, which was the usual practice for butchers until regulations took hold. This business later moved down the street, close to the Town Hall, where one of the sons continued to run it for some years. In 1841, there were ten families living here, consisting of thirty-seven people. William Penrose, his wife, and son, Henry, were residents, as were

The High Street in 1900. Tewkesbury is looking a little like the Wild West with a horseman trotting up the street.

Thomas Mann, who was sixty-five years old, along with his wife, and a girl of two years, who was possibly a granddaughter. There was also a family living in the alley called Matty, which is another old Tewkesbury family name.

By 1851 there were eleven families, the Matty family being one of them. In the 1861 census, only one family was recorded; John Perkins, a waterman from Forthampton, with his wife and a niece, Sarah Ann, who was a 'silk thrower'.

Rent for these cottages could vary; in 1910 Henry Green rented a cottage with a bedroom on each of two floors and a kitchen on the ground floor, at 9d, per week. It was reported to be 'in bad order'. Further along the alley lived George Hallings, whose cottage was costing him 5s 11d, per week. It was the same size but was obviously in better condition.

## Red Lion Alley

The Red Lion was, of course, a pub at what was Nos 84–85 High Street, almost directly opposite Red Lane. Prior to this, the pub was called The Unicorn, and consequently, the alley was Unicorn Alley. The pub was in existence for some thirty years, until 1867. The last

This is one of the alleys demolished in 1965 on the upper High Street. Close to this would have been the Unicorn and later, the Red Lion Pub. This view looks towards the High Street.

landlord was Joseph Walker, the father of Thomas Walker, who had the large engineering works in Oldbury Road. Latterly, the reputation of this establishment suffered, with John Rogers stating that rumours of haunting were spread about the town after all the wickedness that went on there. Later, in around 1870, the premises were demolished and two new houses were built on the site, which survived until the 1965 clearance.

It is possible that this alley could also have been Workhouse Alley, as the buildings were used for a short time by one of the religious orders in the town, to provide accommodation for the more unfortunate members of society.

In 1841, there were seven families in the alley. William Woodward was a sixty-five-year-old barber, with a wife, and a son aged fifteen. Ten years on and Mr Woodward is now seventy-seven years old, (who kept count then!). The Landlord of the pub is now Mr Edwin Merrick, and at this time, he has two hawkers staying there.

In 1861 George Walker is recorded as a waterman and an innkeeper, and the only other resident, apart from his wife, is John Woodward, a brewer, who is possibly the son of William Woodward.

A record dated 1851 states that the contents of the Red Lion were sold for £39 10s 6d, to Weaver and Moore, Auctioneers.

## Unicorn Alley

The alley also known as the Red Lion Alley *(see previous entry)*.

## Steels Court

This court stood between Nos 84 and 85 High Street, the area that was demolished in 1965, and was one of the courts with just a few cottages. The court ran almost through to Oldbury

Road. In 1841 there were four of these in occupation, and just fourteen people living there. Richard Musson was a seventy-year-old stocking-maker, with a daughter aged fifty and a granddaughter aged twenty. In 1913, Thomas Walker of Oldbury Road, owned a cottage here, which was rented to a Miss George, at £4 10s per annum.

## Castles Alley

Thomas Walker owned some of the cottages in 1913, one of which was rented to a Miss George at £4 10s per annum. This had two bedrooms, a kitchen and living room and external facilities, shared of course. Castles Alley was only one of the names given to Double Alley.

## Double Alley

This is the alley that springs to mind whenever alleys are mentioned in the town, because of its notoriety. It earned a poor reputation because of the residents' propensity for a regular drink at weekends! This should not be too heavy a criticism, however, as the density of the housing, the large population living in the crowded hosing, and the dreadful sanitation conditions, must have driven most of these residents to despair.

Shop fronts in the
High Street c.1871.

The alley was sited at Nos 87-88 High Street, and held the dubious honour of having no less than four different names: Castles Alley, Harris's Alley, and the official name, Oldbury Walk. This has a more peaceful and relaxed ring to it, however hardly anyone ever used the name, and it was always Double Alley!

In 1841, there were twenty families living, or should it be surviving, here. This made a total of ninety people, with a wide variety of occupations. From waterman and bricklayer, to a lady called Sarah Anderson, aged eighty as classed as a Brewer! It was not unusual for grandchildren to live with grandparents, and Sarah had two with her. William Collins, a twenty-year-old bricklayer, had a wife who was also twenty, and three children; they were obviously early starters. George Evans, a Whitesmith, lived in the end house on the north side, with his wife, three sons and a daughter.

Ten years later, in 1851, there were thirteen families and a total of ninety souls still here. Five of the families of the previous census are still resident: William Collins is still laying bricks around the town, and could be the family to whom John Rogers refers in his book. William Devereux is seventy-one years old and is a farm labourer. His wife is the same age and is classed as a Pauper. In 1841, the son Thomas was twenty-five, but is now thirty-nine, an indication perhaps, that records were not so important then.

The *Tewkesbury Register*, in February 1857, reported that in order to abate a nuisance, it would be necessary to cover a portion of the open drain and remove the 'trap', placed further up the alley. This is confirmation of the channels which ran through some of the alleys at this time.

There were various owners of the premises in the alley; Mr R.Green Snr and Janet Jones of Pembridge House, High Street were just two. There was the usual single bedroom on each of two floors, a kitchen and pantry, and shared washhouse and WC and garden up the alley. All this was for a rental of 1s 9d for Mr Amphlett, to 2s 3d, for Mr Hathaway.

To compound the problem of overcrowding, the *Tewkesbury Register* reported on the 29 April 1922, that George Smith had been given a licence to keep a Lodging House in the alley.

At the Oldbury Road end of the alley, was a building called Foresters Hall, which may have been the property of one of the religious organisations and used as a kind of alms house.

## Harris Alley

The alley of many names: Double, Castles and Oldbury Walk.

## Oldbury Walk

The official name for Double Alley.

## Glovers Alley

One of the alleys which disappeared in the reconstruction of the upper High Street in 1965, this one was located at Nos 88-89 High Street, adjacent to Double Alley but without its reputation.

The Black Bear pub is reputed to be the oldest in Gloucestershire and uses the Bear and Ragged Staff of Warwickshire as its sign.

Two other names applied to this alley too: Mansells Alley and Townsends Alley, which were both apparently family names, and it may well have been Strawfords Court. John Rogers says that there were twelve houses and the census of 1841 shows eleven families in residence with forty-eight people – a well-populated area. There were also two houses unoccupied at this time.

The population fluctuated over the years, and by 1861 only seven families lived here. However, by 1871, all twelve premises were occupied again, and fifty-nine people were here. Ten years later, William White, his wife and two children are recorded and the family is still here but there are now eight in the family. Another cottage houses the Tyrley family who have a son who is twelve years old, and is an 'errand boy'. He was born a long way from home in Ripon, Yorkshire.

Mr E.P. Gurney was renting here in 1910, and paying 2s for two bedrooms, a kitchen and shared external facilities.

## Mansells Court

Glovers Alley and Townsends Alley are two names that have been in use at Nos 88-89 High Street, until the area was swept away in 1965.

## Townsends Alley

This was known as Mansells and Glovers Alley. A report from the *Tewkesbury Register* tells us that Charles Wharton died of cholera here, in 1849. He was a weaver, with a wife and one daughter.

## Bronds Court

This court was next down the High Street from Glovers Alley, and got its name from the plumber who lived on the front house in the latter part of the nineteenth century. There is some uncertainty about this name, which may be Broads Court.

## Mayalls Court

This is a family name, which has been known in Tewkesbury for many generations. This one refers to a Christopher Mayall, present in the early nineteenth century. Never very heavily populated, in the 1841 census there were only two families in this alley: Woodward and Taylor. Elizabeth Woodward was named as the head of the family, with three sons and a daughter. Ten years later, only the Woodwards remain, and the head is now Thomas, aged forty-five, with Elizabeth, indicating that he was away from home at the last census. The Codrington family owned the properties in 1854.

In 1861 three families are in occupation. Jesse Gregory, a waterman aged twenty-six, lived here. He became the lock keeper in later life, living in the old lock keepers house on the river. At this time, Christopher Mayall is recorded as a gardener and greengrocer, which meant a change of course along the way.

By 1881 only two families are here: Martha Savage, a waterman's wife, and William Hawker another waterman aged fifty-two.

## Waldrons Court

This was a court located at Nos 90-91 High Street, so called after Mr Waldron, who owned property here in the early part of the nineteenth century. In 1841 it was called an alley, indicating a through passage to Oldbury Road. There were nine families there at this date; one was the Holland family. The family included the father, James, his wife and three children. The eldest, William, worked as a waterman but died of cholera in 1849.

The Happy Return Cottages were listed in this alley when a valuation took place in 1910, and were owned by Arnold Perrett. (The Happy Returns was a public house on this site from at least 1869 to 1915, so this may be the connection of the names.) Mrs Hawker rented one with two small bedrooms and a kitchen, and also shared the usual offices and a yard, all for 2s 2d per week.

## Sun Alley

Built in an area of the town that has seen many changes, Sun Alley was built alongside the Rising Sun Inn and was located close to where the old Tewkesbury railway station would have been. In 1841 there were five families here, twenty-seven people in all, one of whom was William Crump, who was still making stockings at ninety years of age. Francis Chapman was listed as a chair maker, living on his own. Linnel states that there was a private road from the High Street to Oldbury Road, giving access to the stables and other outbuildings. The line of Sun Street indicated this location before the demolition of the area took place.

The upper High Street (*above*) before the wholesale demolition of the area in 1965-66 and further down the High Street (*below*) is Mayalls Court and Waldrons Court.

The passage into the Oddfellows Pub ran along the left hand side of the building and so into the bar. The location was No. 110 High Street, which is now a shoe shop.

## Oddfellows Passage

The Oddfellows Arms was another of the town's pubs that has gone, the site now being occupied by a shoe shop at No. 109 High Street. The building still retains the pub's glazed brick pillars at each side of the shop. Access to the bar was along a passage to the left of the frontage. This pub closed in 1971 and the passage went when the building was altered.

## Hodges Alley

This was an earlier name for Eagles Alley, which still exists, and was recorded as Hodges Alley in *c.*1750.

## Roberts Court

Recorded in the 1910 Valuations, this court lay behind the Roberts Brothers shop at No. 112 High Street, next to Osborne's Garage. William Henry Roberts was living at the shop, but at the rear of the property stood a bake house, harness room, a loose box, store room and a pig sty, which made it quite a substantial property. The rent was recorded at £3 18s 4d per annum. It was probably just a small area with only one property in it.

## Codringtons Alley

A name, which will be familiar to most people in the town, as Sir William Codrington was an MP for the town from 1761 to 1790. The alley was situated at Nos 118–119 High Street, between what is now The Bakers Oven and a Mr Minit shop. The Codrington family owned extensive properties in the town, particularly in the alleys.

## Clothiers Alley

A name which could have derived from an occupation, but there seems to be no evidence for this. However, the name by which it was more familiarly known was Scotts Alley.

## Scotts Alley

An alternative name for this alley was Clothiers Alley *(see previous entry)*, possibly reflecting the occupation of the frontager. This was sited between Nos 122 and 123 High Street, and was later known as Scott's Alley. Joseph Scott had his ironmongers business here, with workshops down the alley; John Rogers calls him a whitesmith and bell hanger. The alley went through to Oldbury Road, but the High Street entrance was stopped at the time Rogers writes.

It is possible to see remains of the alley at the rear of the houses in Trinity Street, but the last two houses were at the Oldbury Road end and were demolished by Sweets, the builders in around 1950, to make way for the garage which is still there.

The Poor Rate Assessment of 1840, shows sixteen families in the alley, but at the 1841 census, there is a record of only six families resident, which is a problem that requires further investigation – where had ten families gone in just one year?

One of the families was that of John Everiss, a bleacher living with his wife, daughter and grandson. Ten years later, at the age of sixty-nine, he is referred to as a 'pauper, who is reliant on the parish'.

In 1861 there were still six houses occupied. John Everiss is now eighty-one, and is a widower, with two daughters at home. Two of the other families have the name of Pilley: Edward is sixty-two and a widower, while Gurney Pilley and his sister are thirteen and seven respectively, and are probably grandchildren. Much later, a Gurney Pilley became the town crier for Tewkesbury. There is a second family, headed by Francis Pilley, who is aged thirty-eight. He is a mason's labourer, with a wife and a daughter-in-law, both working in the shoe trade.

In 1871 there are only four families here: Edward Pilley is now seventy-one and has a son-in-law living here – Edward Pilley Gurney, a twenty-year-old bricklayer.

Only two houses were occupied by 1881. James Walker is head of one, and is raising a family of nine children, aged one year to twenty years! His wife is only forty-two years of age. William Bulman, 'a retired private coachman', occupies the second house.

The Poll of 1868 records three voters: Enoch Ricketts – a tinman, Thomas Noxon – an ostler, and Thomas Newman – a blacksmith.

In 1910, a valuation of one of the cottages tells us that it is owned by Mrs Henegar and rented to Mr A. Bennett at a weekly rent of 2s 6d per week. There was a bedroom on each of the top two floors, while the ground floor had one living room. Outside there was a shared WC and a washhouse. Two similar cottages were rented to William Newman and Mr

This was Mr Watson's shop, which fronted onto the High Street. After his death, Mr Watson's shop remained closed for a number of years. When it was opened up, the contents were found to be intact and remained the same as when it was as a thriving business.

Portman. Ten years later, the rents were still the same, as were the tenants. Some of the last tenants to live here were the Northey family.

## Haywards Alley

Also known as Malverns Alley, John Rogers calls this Haywards Court, so perhaps there was no entrance at the Oldbury Road end when he wrote his article. The other name used was Malverns Alley, and Rogers also uses Malverns Court. Perhaps the two names were in use at the same time during a transitional period.

The passage still runs between Haywards hardware shop and its neighbour on the north side, which is a shop that also belonged to Haywards for many years, and on through to Oldbury Road.

There were several cottages in the alley, typical of the two and three storey cottages in other alleys. These were used as workshops for many years by Haywards before their main workshop was built. It is still possible to see one of these cottages.

## Malverns Alley

The alternative name for Haywards Alley *(see previous entry)*.

## Sperrys Alley

This was a previous name for Walls Court *(see p41)*.

## Heaths Alley

At around the turn of the twentieth century, Mr Heath ran his bakers business at Nos 130-131 High Street. However, one report has the alley closed by 1910, but in September 1919, the *Tewkesbury Register* recorded that George Thomas was fined 5s, for riding his bicycle along this alley. Perhaps just the High Street end was closed. Mr Heath was in business for quite some time as a Police Court report of 1882, states that 'Thomas Smith, aged twelve, was caught stealing 3s 7d from Walter Heath's bakers shop'. He spent one night in prison and received four strokes of the birch.

## Wheatsheaf Passage

This is still in existence, and can be seen to the left of No. 132 High Street .The building that was the Wheatsheaf public house from the late eighteenth century until its closure in 1956, is at present an antique shop. This passage would have given access to the rear of the pub where there was a skittle alley, a pre-requisite for most pubs in the town. Bennett's *History of Tewkesbury* states that there was a 'fives court' (this is similar to a squash court, but is open, with only three sides), and at one time a 'cockpit' here.

## Lanes Alley

Another alley with a family name, this was located close to No. 135 High Street. In 1841 there was just one family living here: a plumber by the name of Francis West, aged thirty, with a wife and two daughters.

The Wheatsheaf Inn, with the door to the passage closed, but advertising a 'Good teak skittle alley at the rear' on the door.

A view of the lower part of High Street in c. 1870. The entrance to Culls Alley can just be seen on the right hand side of the picture.

## Culls Alley

In 1856 James Cull had his plumbing business located at Nos 139-140 High Street. The entrance would have been somewhere between the south side of Alison's Bookshop and Clarence House. The alley was demolished in around 1956.

## Collins Alley

This is in the upper part of the High Street and refers to a bricklayer/builder by the name of Collins.

## Gotheridges Alley

There is little information on this alley. Linnel records that the name was used as early as 1777, but that it was extinguished in around 1869.

## Predys Court

This was also known as Wadleys Court in the eighteenth century.

## Wadleys Alley

Previously called Predys Alley *(see previous entry)*.

## Strawfords Alley

In the High Street, possibly named after a local beadle of that name, who probably lived at the upper end of the High Street.

CHAPTER FIVE
# Barton Street

## Tysoes Passage

This is not strictly an alley but is worth recording as most people will remember the shop at Nos 5-7 Barton Street. The adverts in the town guides over many years show the passage on the right hand side of the shop, probably leading to the storerooms. Tysoe's were in business here for more than a hundred years, closing in the 1940s.

## Millards Court

Just around the corner of the High Street, at Nos 6-7 Barton Street, was Millards Court. However, when Mr Millard left the town in around 1835, this became Gardners Court, as a Mrs Gardner owned the front house and some of the cottages. There would appear to have been three cottages here, and in 1841, Thomas Noxon, a name that has cropped up before as living in at least two other alleys, was living here with a wife and six children. Stephen Close is also in residence, and is a labourer with a wife and three children.

Ten years later, Mr Noxon has passed away and his widow is classed as a pauper, despite having three children at work, and a lodger who is also a pauper. Mr Close is still living here with just one daughter at home now. By 1861 she has left and there are two lodgers in the house.

The three cottages are occupied through to 1891, with Thomas Howse and his family living in one. The poll of 1868 records only two voters: Henry Harding and Thomas Howse, a tailor.

## Crooked Alley

This was so called because of its structure: there were five bends in the alley, from Barton Street to Oldbury Road. Before the Nelson Street was opened up, this was the main route through to Oldbury Road. Part of this alley remains as Alexander Court, with a doorway off Barton Street, while the entrance to Oldbury Road can still be seen, at the corner of Oldbury Road and Nelson Street. John Rogers records that there was hat manufacturing taking place, a business owned by Mr Holland. Further down the alley was a framesmith's workshop, where stocking machines were repaired.

*Left:* The entrance to what was Crooked Alley, leading from Barton Street.

*Opposite above:* The entrance to Huntleys Court can be seen on the right of the photograph. At this time the court was closed off.

*Opposite below:* A wartime photograph of ARP wardens marching along Barton Street. The building in the background is the Nelson Inn and on the left hand side of the Inn is a door into Huntleys Court.

## Huntleys Court

This court was located quite close to the Nelson public house, and has now been demolished to widen the street through to Oldbury Road. Thomas Huntley was a baker, with a shop on the front street, for some fifty years. The passage ran through into an open courtyard and then passed on into Oldbury Road. In the courtyard was a communal hand water pump, for the use of the residents. This facility was in use well into the 1940 period, according to a family that lived there. Since the demolition of that area, there is no trace of the alley.

The shop was eventually taken by a Mrs Driscoll, who sold groceries. She also owned most of the property in the court during the 1930s.

In *Slater's Directory* for 1850, Thomas Huntley was aged fifty-seven and referred to as a baker and beer-seller, with a wife and two daughters and one son. Beer houses were common in the town for many years, and houses for sale were usually sold 'with brew house'.

## Nelson Alley

An alley obviously located alongside the Nelson public house, of which John Rogers states 'for some years the thoroughfare has been stopped as it is all private property', indicating that there was probably an access through to Oldbury Road at one stage.

In 1841, it was a well-populated area with twelve houses, ten of them being occupied with thirty-three people in residence. John (Pony) Hyett was the Innkeeper, aged seventy-five at

that time. During his youth, he had worked at the Old Star and Garter Coaching Inn, in what is now Chapel Court, and probably learned the trade there.

Perhaps because of the density of the population in the alley, the cholera epidemic of 1832, took eight victims from this alley, between 21 August and 30 August. These included four children between the ages of two and six years.

## Nailors Alley

It is likely that this alley was located near to the present day Nelson Street, and as the name implies, was filled with people working in the nail-making trade. The majority of the property, if not all, was owned by an ironmonger, Samuel Barnes, who was in business for many years. He was also responsible for building Barnes Almshouses in Chance Street, which is now demolished. Spring Gardens sheltered accommodation is built on the site. The alley was demolished in the early part of the nineteenth century to provide the road from Barton Street to Oldbury Road.

## Morris Alley

In 1905 there were six houses in the alley, which, according to John Rogers, were 'built in the very old style', and were poor, dark and small cottages. The alley was in the area of what is now Nelson Street.

## Harewoods Alley

This is another of the alleys with two names. Mr Harewood was recorded here in the early 1800s, but this is now called Charlewoods Alley, (not Charleswoods as the sign tells us), and lies next to the police station. In 1841 there were seven families living here.

## Thomas Alley

In the 1841 census, Mary Thomas lived here and had a pawnbroking business. This is the only record found so far of this alley.

## Collins Court

This is an alley that has caused some confusion by its association with Longs Alley, but in the 1841–1861 census returns it is situated at Nos 26–27 Barton Street. The census of 1841 shows that Edmund Collins, a thirty-three-year-old bricklayer was resident here, at No. 27. In the 1861 census there were four families living in the court, including Samuel Collins, aged sixty-one, who was a stocking weaver, and his wife Maria, aged sixty-five, who was a washerwoman, an occupation that was quite common in the town.

At the time of the 1868 Census, there were only two voters registered in the alley: James King, a hay trusser, and James McDonald, a labourer.

In 1910, a valuation of the properties in the alley showed that the rent varied from 1s 5d per week, to 2s 8d per week. This would be for a cottage with one bedroom, a kitchen and a shared WC and washhouse outside. At this time one Louise Roberts owned the property.

## Longs Alley

This is now demolished. The name was given to the alley at Nos 26–27 Barton Street, but it was also known as Collins Court after a builder, Edmund Collins, who lived at the front and owned some of the property in the court. It was here that a couple of the cottages were built together to form one of the first Wesleyan Chapels in the town. It has long been the view that John Wesley preached here, as did George Whitfield, the preacher from Gloucester, and that when the chapel was full, they made use of the meadow of Joe Hughes, of Hughes Alley, on Perry Hill. When the Wesleyan Chapel was built at Tolsey Lane, these two reverted to dwellings again.

## Costnetts Alley

This is the present day Woods Court at Nos 35–36 Barton Street. Originally it would have passed through to East Street, but now of course it is just an access to the property in the alley. The valuation of 1910 shows that these houses had one bedroom, a kitchen on the ground floor, and a shared WC and water-pump in the yard. The rents were 2s per week for two of the residents – Mr A. Cumberlin and Mr T. Smith, whose names are recorded in a valuation of 1910.

In 1861 three families lived here: George Barratt aged twenty-three, and classed as a cordwainer, with a wife and two small children, and Thomas Harris who was seventy-three years old and also a cordwainer.

## Whites Court

This court was located at the rear of No. 49 Barton Street and was not in existence for many years. A valuation dated 1910, shows only one cottage there, which was unoccupied. Alfred Mayall owned it and the rent was set at 2s 6d per week. This was a two storied house with two bedrooms, a kitchen and a back kitchen, (scullery), and a shared outside WC and washhouse, indicating that there were some other residents in the area.

## Freemans Court

This court was located next to the old Congregational church, which is now the Church of The Latter Day Saints, in Barton Street, and was built by George Freeman, the owner of the factory in East Street. He lived at No. 63 Barton Street and in his will he left the property to the Trustees of the Independent Chapel, providing that the right of way to the side entrance of the chapel was retained. The houses in Orchard Court backed onto this area.

In 1851 there were five families living in the court: Susannah Golding was a bonnet maker, an occupation that crops up regularly. Samuel Mayall was a forty-four-year-old carpenter, with a wife and three children. Emma was sixteen and a teacher's assistant. Alfred, at fourteen

The map of 1883, showing the location of Wrights Court and Freemans Court on opposite sides of Barton Street.

was a tailor's apprentice, all indicating a well educated and aspiring family, which remained living here for the next twenty years.

By the time of the next census in 1861, Susannah Golding is still a bonnet maker, aged sixty-six! Mr Mayall has lost his wife, and his daughter Susan is now his housekeeper. At this date, two houses are empty with the residents 'Absent on Sunday Night', according to the census.

By 1891 there are five houses occupied: Joseph Taylor has lived here for the past thirty years and is eighty-four years old, and still recorded as an agricultural labourer. In another cottage Lewis Collins has a wife aged forty-seven, and nine children aged from seven months to nineteen years! In a valuation of 1925, these houses were rented at 4s 6d per week.

There were families resident here at the outbreak of the second war, but the houses were demolished shortly after this. The wall of the chapel is still whitewashed, indicating the alleyway, or part of the open area.

## Parkers Court

This court was located at Nos 56-57 Barton Street and had nine cottages. By the 1841 census, however, only four of them were occupied. Ten years later all nine were rented out and there were twenty-two people in the court. At this time, Charles Desborough was aged sixty-six and recorded as a Greenwich (Chelsea?), Pensioner. Oddly, in the same court, Samuel Leonard, also sixty-six, was also recorded as a Chelsea Pensioner, born in Tewkesbury. Was this a coincidence, or were they comrades in arms?

By 1861, there was an increase in the population in the court, from twenty-two to thirty-three, and one third of these were under ten years of age. Thomas Dibble aged thirty-four, lived here with a wife and four children, and ten years later, the census records that he was still here, with four children at home and a lodger in residence.

There were nine families, with a total of fifty people. James Moseley, a forty-year-old cordwainer was doing his bit to boost the population, with eight children. Two of them were in the same trade!

In 1881 all nine cottages are filled. James Moseley, at fifty, has only two children at home. One James Atwood, (another familiar name), is fifty-nine years old and has a wife, thirty-nine, and six children. They were obviously late starters! Ten years later he is still in the court with only three children at home.

In the 1868 poll there were only three voters: Thomas Drinkwater and James Moseley, both shoemakers, and John Parsons, a framework knitter.

In 1920, the houses were rented out, at between 1s 9d and 3s per week, by Mrs Mayall of No. 39 Barton Street.

## Finchers Alley

Now gone and built over, this alley was situated where Nos 57-58 Barton Street now stands. John Fincher was a baker with his business here in 1840. In 1851 there were five families resident, with a total of seventeen people. Robert Woodward is a thirty-two-year-old stocking maker, living with his wife, a daughter and a mother-in-law who is aged seventy-one. In the 1861 census, there are only three families with a total of thirteen people. Mr Woodward is still in residence, and now has a son, Alfred, aged five.

Ten years later we see one cottage empty but three are still occupied. Mr Woodward is now fifty-three years old and still making stockings. By 1881 only one family resides here: John Noxon and his wife Joan. This John Noxon had been living in Culls Alley in 1868.

These buildings were demolished later to make way for new houses at the front of the street.

## Burrows Court

The site of this court presents a little difficulty, in that Linnel has it at Nos 58-59 Barton street, but a deed for the sale of the present day museum building has a plan which shows the court placed between this property and the shop which is now a newspaper and sweet shop, Nos 63-64 Barton Street. This is the more likely site, as there is an entrance between the two leading to an open area, probably a courtyard, and currently giving access to the rear. Linnel states further that in 1853, at Nos 58-59, there was a barber here named John Burrows.

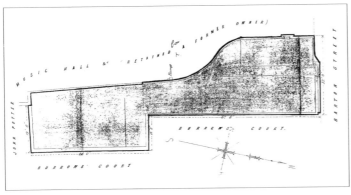

*Above:* Burrows Court in around 1920. It lies between the museum building and the small shop on the left.

*Left:* From a deed held in the museum, this plan shows the entrance from Barton Street into Burrows Court.

## Whiteheads Court

This court was located at Nos 61-62 Barton Street, but I can find no other information on what is a family named court.

## Evans Alley

The entrance to this alley, previously known as Pullocks Alley, is still at Nos 67–68 Barton Street. There is a peculiarity at the entrance to this alley at the left; the wall has been cut away at about three feet from the ground. While there is no recorded reason for this, it could be that in order to deliver goods to the workshop in the alley, the wall was cut away. Mr Evans was a nail maker who had a workshop in the alley, so this explanation may have some basis in fact.

In 1851 there were nine cottages in the alley, so life here must have been hectic with all the movement of people. This alley would have led on to Saffron Road.

## Pullocks Alley
Recorded earlier as Evans Alley *(see previous entry)*.

## Peacheys Court
Another of the smaller courts in the town, this one was accessed directly off Nos 71-72 Barton Street, and was demolished to make way for the National Westminster Bank in around 1969. Mr Peachey was a builder/carpenter, who lived here in around 1840, according to Linnel.

In 1871 there were seven families here comprising thirty-six people. George Hewitt, aged thirty-five and a labourer, has a wife and six children; one son William is a 'pot boy', at one of the many pubs. Could this be one of the forebears of the Hewitt's who were in business in Church Street? William Wilkes is sixty-seven and lives with his wife and two daughters, and also has two lodgers.

*Left:* The entrance to Burrows Court between the Museum and a small shop.

*Right:* The entrance to Whiteheads Court, on the south side of Barton Street. The cottages are gone but the alley remains.

In 1881 there are only four families in residence. Mr Wilkes is now seventy-seven, his daughter is fifty-one and a nurse, and one of his boarders age fourteen is called a 'nurses girl', perhaps influenced by the daughter.

## Workhouse Alley

Recorded at several locations in the town at different times, this alley in Barton Street refers to the existing Fish Alley. There was a bag-making workshop at the bottom end of the alley, which perhaps gave the name. There are references to Red Lion Alley, Unicorn Alley, and Hughes Alley, having the same name. The practice of the Union Workhouse giving out work to be done in the town, may have given rise to some of these locations having this name.

## Joyces Alley

An alley, which has been known by three different names, it is now known as Fish Alley, at Nos 69-70 Barton Street. Joyces and Bells Alley were the names given after two ladies who lived here at different times. The more recent names were Fish Alley East and Fish Alley West, applied to the top and bottom of the alley, which leads down to the Swilgate Road.

## Myrtle Court

A small court, which was accessed from Hughes Alley and contained six small cottages. In 1924, Emily Summers rented one of these at £2 12s per annum, from Mr Howells, of Coutts and Howells, Builders of Barton Street. This court was adjacent to Peacheys Court, which was accessed from Barton Street.

## Greens Court

This is located at Nos 81-82 Barton Street and is still extant, known now by the name of Masons Court. William Green was a tailor living in the shop facing the street in 1840.

## Gannaways Court

The poll book of 1868 shows that John Gannaway was a butcher living here. By 1881 we see his widow, Honor Gannaway, still here at the age of seventy-seven, supported by her children. Her daughter, aged forty-one and also named Honor, is married to Edwin Pullin, who is aged fifty-three, and is also a butcher, probably carrying on the business started by his father-in-law.

# CHAPTER SIX

# Church Street South

## Harris Alley

This is another alley that had more than one name in the nineteenth century. Benjamin Harris had a Corn Merchants business here. Located at The Cross end of the street, at Nos 4–5, it has also been recorded as Mathews Alley after the butchers shop of that name.

## Quart Pot Alley

The Quart Pot was a hostelry, which stood next to the Methodist church at The Cross. The alleyway ran alongside the pub and down toward Swilgate Road providing stabling and other facilities.

## Savings Bank Alley

This is the other name for the previous alley – the Quart Pot Alley, as the later building became a bank. The Savings Bank name can be seen on the first floor window.

## Bubbs Alley

The only mention of this alley I have been able to find, is in Norah Day's book, *They Lived in Tewkesbury*. The alley appears to have been either Ancills Court or Lilleys Alley. The likelihood is that the name Bubb was applied for just a short time. The census of 1841 records that Benjamin Bubb was living at No. 56 High Street, and worked as a musician. There is no other indication that there was any relationship between the two.

## Packers Court

The owner of several properties in this area of Church Street was a man by the name of John 'Corkleg' Packer, so called because he had a cork or wooden leg. He gave his name to the court at Nos 10–11 Church Street. In 1835 he was renting a shop further down the street to a widow by the name of Mary Lilley, hence the name of this alley. Mr Packer was a hosier with a thriving business in the town.

*Above:* Church Street looking at The Cross. The cars on the left tell us that this is around 1930 and the gas lamps are still in use.

*Below left:* Packers Court sited at Nos 10-11 Church Street.

*Below centre:* This is Nicholls Alley, with the doorway from Church Street.

*Below right:* Nicholls Alley, Church Street.

*Above:* Church Street at The Cross with Barnett's Restaurant on the left, in the early 1950s.

*Left:* No 24 Nicholls Alley from Swilgate Road and looking towards Church Street. This shows the alley leading down to Swilgate Brook.

## Nicholls Alley

Open the doorway at Nos 18-19 Church Street, and it is possible to see this old alley, with the blue brick floor and the right hand wall whitewashed, all the way down to Swilgate Road. In 1841 there were five families recorded in the census returns, consisting of just twelve people having a variety of trades.

## Aurora Passage

The passage carries the name of the pub or beer house located at No. 36 Church Street. The passage is still there and has a gate restricting entry. The passage is also recorded as Buckles Court in the census returns for 1861-1881, with Charles Buckle as a Brewer-Innkeeper of the Aurora. In 1861 there were two houses at the end of the passage, one of which was occupied by George Knight, who was a butcher, aged thirty-four. He had a wife, Ann, and a daughter aged seven. His twenty-five year-old brother, Charles, also lived there, and was a saddler by trade. In 1871, Mr Buckle is still Landlord at the age of fifty-two. This conflicts with Brian Linnell's record of his tenancy ending in 1869.

At this time there are still two families living here: a miller called William Mayall, a name that crops up time and time again, and George Mitchell, a boot maker with a wife and two children.

Aurora Passage: part of the medieval row of cottages in Church Street.

It would appear that the named changed after this as the census of 1881 records it as Aurora Passage.

In the 1930s, there were still two families living at this address: Woolley and Drinkwater, and information of these families was given by Kathleen Woolley.

## Whiteheads Alley

An alternative name for the Aurora Passage *(see previous entry)*.

## Gibbs Court

This was the entrance to Barsanti's Abbey Tea Gardens in Church Street. John Rogers states that 'Mr Gibbs carried on the business of a Baker'. This would have been before the tea gardens were established. There were apparently several cottages in the court, which had a rear view of the abbey, but I can find no mention of the occupants, so perhaps this was a short lived description of the court.

## Woodwards Alley

An alternative name for Finches Alley.

These are the Edward Richardson Almshouses in Gander Lane, off Church Street. They were built for the poor of the town in 1651.

# CHAPTER SEVEN

# Oldbury Road

OLDBURY ROAD DEFINES THE AREA of the town that was undeveloped before the Enclosures Act of 1808 was passed, with the road running parallel with the High Street. The map of 1793, published by Dyde, clearly demonstrates the extent of the town before this development took place on the Oldbury Fields.

The OS map of 1903, shows how the town was extended, covering all of this area, including Rope Walk, almost to the site of the present Safeway supermarket.

The area along Oldbury Road has seen many changes, with the building of the Trinity Church, Walkers Engineering Works and the cattle markets. More recently, the demolition of Spring Gardens, the building of the Cascades Pool and the removal of Warner's Garages to make way for car parking, has forced changes in this area.

## Alexander Place

This was the end of Crooked Alley, which came from Barton Street and into Oldbury Road. This end of the alley can still be seen today, from the corner of Nelson Street and Oldbury Road.

## Merretts Yard

This yard can be seen on most of the earlier OS maps, and is almost opposite the entrance to East Street from Nelson Street, with the yard backing on to the High Street. The area takes its name from a butcher who had a business on the High Street.

In 1841 there were eight families living here, mostly employed in the stocking-making or the lace-making industry. Thomas Holbrook, however, was a butcher, (working for Mr Merrett perhaps), and was thirty years old with a wife aged forty and a family of six children, the oldest being fifteen years of age.

In a letter from the local board of health, the occupants of the yard were ordered to construct a drain 'to specification', to communicate with the main drain owned by the

*Opposite:* This is the seventeenth century building in Walls Court, which was saved from destruction by a small local trust called Gem Towns. It was then renovated to become a superb dwelling again.

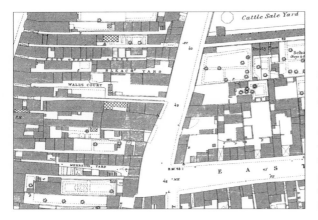

*Left:* This map of 1883 shows the location of both Bleach Yard and Merretts Yard in Oldbury Road.

*Opposite:* Walls Court is actually an alley that goes through the Oldbury. This leads towards the High Street and gives a clear picture of how the alleys were developed, with timber-framed buildings and later brick tenements.

council, and were given fourteen days to comply. At the same time the owners of Gravel Walk were sent the same direction, but only had seven days notice. This was in keeping with the local authority attempting to clean up the town.

The 1868 poll recorded six voters living here. In 1910 a series of valuations showed that cottages No. 1 to No. 3 were empty, while the rents of Nos 4 to 9 varied from 1s 8d per week, to 2s 3d per week. These were houses with one bedroom on each of two floors, a kitchen and a pantry on the ground floor, and a shared outside WC.

In the period prior to and just after the last war, according to information from Mr Bert Avery, the Avery and Garfield families were just two of the families living here.

## Bleach Yard

Located between Old Post Office Alley and Walls Court, this was an area that took its name from the stocking-making industry. The finished stockings, because of their brown colour, were bleached to whiten them for sale to the public. The access to the yard was from Oldbury Road.

In the census of 1841 there were five cottages, four of which were occupied. In 1860, these five were sold to George Watson, Draper, for £400, this sum being borrowed from Thomas Walker of Oldbury Road, and repaid in 1875. Later that year, C.E. Edgecumbe of Hanley Castle, sold a warehouse and five cottages to Thomas Walker for £460.

Thomas Walker continued to wheel and deal, for in 1880, he sold the properties to William Knight, who took out a mortgage of £500 at 5% interest. Two years later, the warehouse had become a cottage again, earning a weekly rent.

In 1910, a valuation showed that the six premises were again in the ownership of Thomas Walker. Five of them were occupied, and bringing in a rent of between 1s 6d and 2s 6d per week, with the sixth cottage now being used as a storage unit. The houses had two bedrooms, a living room on the ground floor, and a shared WC and washhouse outside in the yard.

In 1922, fire insurance was taken out by Mary Hannah Collins Walker, the owner, who lived at Ferndale, a house next to the hospital in Barton Street.

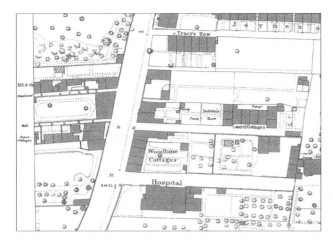

The same map showing the top of Oldbury Road, with Dobbins Row leading off Old Hospital Lane.

## Dobbins Row

This was a row of houses located between Tracy Row and Hollams Road in Oldbury Road. Named after a butcher who had his business in the High Street, Dobbins Row consisted of a small terrace of three houses. The OS map of 1883 shows these properties with a small garden, some way back from the Oldbury Road, and surprisingly, a water pump in the yard.

In 1906, a valuation tells us that Mrs Wardell-Yerbough, the wife of the incumbent at the Abbey, owned them. The rent for the house occupied by Mr Thomas Hall, was 1s 7d per week. The houses were demolished in 1909.

## Hansfords Court

Also known as Wrights Court after the family who owned the property, this was located in East Street. Hansford was in fact a frame smith in the nineteenth century, and owned the property through to Barton Street. A valuation of 1910, states that there were four cottages in the court, owned by Miss Mayall, of No. 39 Barton Street. Sarah Wagstaff rented one at 2s 6d per week, Sam Crockett and Harriett Buckle paid 1s 6d per week and Mrs Philpotts was also being charged 1s 6d. John Rogers states that the alley was closed off at Barton Street in 1905.

## Dallingers Court

Unfortunately, John Rogers only records this court as having six houses in it, but gives no other information.

## School Court

Refers to the area around Trinity School, an infants school built by the Trinity church and accessed from Oldbury Road via Trinity Walk. The school is now a Masonic Hall.

## Wellington Court

Located somewhere in Oldbury Road, but not yet found.

# CHAPTER EIGHT

# Back of Avon

## Birds Court

At the bottom of Smiths Lane, off the High Street on the south side, there were two small courts. Birds Court had its access from Quay Street South, or Back of Avon as it is now called. The court had six properties, but in 1841, when it was recorded as Birds Alley, only three were occupied. John Bird lived there, with his wife and two children; he was a fifty-year-old framework knitter, a profession that was common in the town.

Ten years later, in 1851, the census showed John Bird still living here, but he is now sixty-six years old. His son-in-law Edward Mew, aged twenty-five, and a daughter-in law Elizabeth Mew, aged sixteen, live with him. There are eight families now, some of them sharing a house, with a total of twenty-six residents. By 1861, only five families were in residence, with one house unoccupied.

In 1871 there were only two families: William Goodwin, with his wife and four children, and Charles Hodges, also with a wife and four offspring. By 1881 William Goodwin, now seventy, has his wife and a grandson, William, who is aged fourteen and is employed as a brick-makers labourer. Charles Hodges is also still in the court, now widowed, but with his eldest daughter and her husband and two sons living there, but not recorded in 1871.

In February 1884, the *Tewkesbury Register* reported that a house in Birds Court, occupied by Thomas Hodges, had been sold to Thomas Clay for £70. Thomas Clay also owned Clays Court in East Street.

The 1891 census tells us that five families occupy the court with one house empty.

## Sweets Court

This area was adjacent to Birds Court and had its access from Smiths Lane. This was another of the smaller courts with just seven houses, all occupied except one in 1851, with twenty-three residents. The main occupation appears to be that of waterman, which is no surprise as it was so close to the river, meaning they could fall out of bed and into work! Lewis Jones, a waterman hailing from Rochdale, was married to Jane Collins. At the time of the 1881

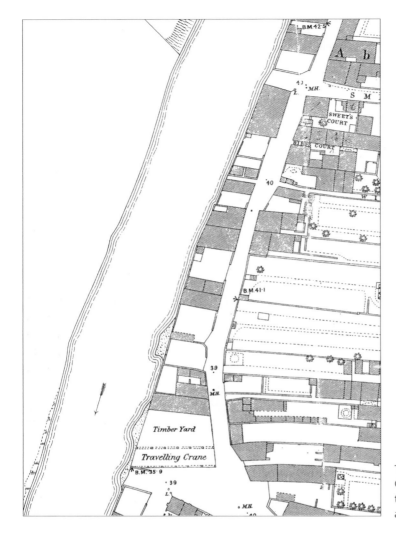

The map shows both Birds Court and Sweets Court at the corner of Smiths Lane and Back of Avon.

census, there were five houses occupied and twenty-five residents. Thomas Halling, another local name, has his wife and four children, and is, yes, a waterman.

Francis Hale, a maltster, lives with his wife, two daughters and a grandson, and remains living here for the next ten years at least. At the time of the 1891 census, he is still a maltster, and his wife is now sixty-two, but she is reported dead at the age of sixty-four in 1895. Ten years later there are only three cottages occupied and only fifteen people in the court. Another waterman, Henry Gregory, is the relative of Jessie Gregory who became the lock keeper later in life, and when he retired, lived on a long-boat on the river.

A valuation taken in 1910 states that 'there are large cellars beneath Sweets Court', indicating perhaps, that there had been an industrial use here, probably associated with the river. The other possibility is that the Hen and Chickens pub had its cellars here.

Information about the residents living here in the mid-nineteenth century has been received from Mrs Edna Fletcher, who lived in the court as a girl. She recalls the names of the King, Portlock, Bishop and Booth families as being residents at this time.

## Catherines Court

Located off Tolsey Lane and on the north side of Priors Alley, this was quite a substantial court, with at least fourteen families there in 1841. Seventy-nine people were residing in this area, which must have been quite a strain on the facilities, if there were any. Benjamin Parker is fifty-five and has a wife, three sons and four lodgers living with him. Sydney Smith is another resident, a chair maker with a family of six children. In 1861 this family had moved to Burrows Court – perhaps the rent was less.

By 1851, only ten families live in the court, and there are four houses recorded as unoccupied. Benjamin Parker is now classed as a pauper at sixty-five years of age.

## Nailors Square

Located at the bottom of Tolsey Lane, the name obviously comes from the nail-making industry, which was thriving in the nineteenth century. Barnes, the ironmonger, provided some of these houses with small forges in their kitchens. This allowed both the husband and wife to carry on the trade. This business was carried on in other parts of the town too – in Evans Alley, Barton Street, for example, as well as Nailors Court in Barton Street. When

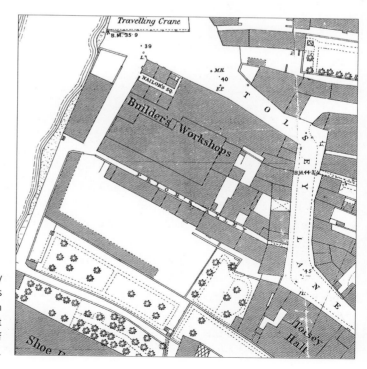

The small squares off Tolsey Lane in 1883. Catherines Court is the large area shown as a builders yard. Rices Court is the small court leading off the north side of Priors Alley.

John Rogers conducted his survey of the houses in the town, he states that there were five properties here. These can be seen on the 1883 OS map.

## Rices Court

Situated between Priors Alley and Catherines Court, this was another area demolished to make way for the building firm of Collins and Godfreys. In 1871 there were only two families living here: William Firth lived at No. 1 with his eighty-two-year-old mother, while Elizabeth Godfrey lived at No. 2. She had two sons at home; Francis and John, one a builders clerk and the other a stonemason. Both were young men who had apparently done well for themselves. There is an anomaly here, in that Linnell states that the court was demolished in around 1850, but there are people recorded here in the 1871 census – perhaps these were the last of the cottages left.

# CHAPTER NINE

# East Street

## Clays Court

Named after a stocking maker, who lived in East Street, the cottages here were built by Thomas Clay. John Rogers records that he was a hard-working man, who eventually owned a lot of property in the town. In the census of 1891 there were three families in the court. Thomas Deveroux was a 'railway servant' working at the railway sheds. James Morse, aged fifty-two, was a labourer with a wife and two daughters, with one working as a 'nurses girl'. James Morse died at the age of fifty-eight in 1899, while still living in this court.

## Wrights Court

Another of the East Street courts on the south side. This court had four cottages, and the OS map of 1883 shows that there was also a water pump at the Barton Street end of the court. A valuation of 1910 shows that Mrs Mayall of No. 39 Barton Street owned the cottages. The residents at this time were Sarah Wagstaff, paying a rent of 2s 6d per week, Sam Crockett and Harriett Buckle paying 1s 6d per week and Mrs Philpotts with a rental of 1s 3d per week.

*Far left:* Wrights Court, 2002. This is all that remains of Wrights Court, situated off Barton Street. Originally this was an alley that went straight through to East Street.

*Left:* Wrights Court, Barton Street.

# CHAPTER TEN

# Unlocated Alleys

THERE ARE SEVERAL NAMES of alleys that have been noted, for which it has not been possible to find a certain location. These are listed below.

## Blizards Court

It is highly likely that this relates to the Blizzard family of Blizzard and Coleman, whose premises were in Quay Street. The name can still be seen on the building, which was taken over in 1863. It may be that there was an entrance to these works, from Quay Street or the Back of Avon for a short while, which had this name.

## Chambers Court

Only two references to this court have been found: one in the report in the *Tewkesbury Register* noted earlier, and one in Bradley-Birt's book on Tewkesbury published in 1931. On the subscription list is the name of Miss Dyer of Chambers Court.

## Johnsons Alley

Unlocated, but possibly in the High Street.

## Reeves Alley or Court

There were two sisters of this name who had a business at The Cross, early in the nineteenth century, but perhaps the name has an earlier origin.

## Lewis Court

The database held at the library, shows that in 1841 there was a Lewis court in Church Street, where Mary Marshall, aged seventy-four, lived. She was a 'lace flowerer', probably working at Freemans factory. Her daughter, aged forty-nine, lived with her, and did the same job.

# CHAPTER ELEVEN

# Existing Alleys

THE STORY OF THE ALLEYS would not be complete without a tour of those alleys and courts which still exist, so the following section will take the reader from Chandlers Court, near the Bell Hotel, along Church Street to The Cross, up the High Street on the left and down on the right, along the north side of Barton Street and back along the south side. Then to The Cross and along Church Street to finish near the Abbey.

## Chandlers Court

This was originally named after Daniel Chandler, a maltster who had his malt house in the court. This is an old family; a descendant still lives at Bredon. Daniel was a collector of the Poor Rate for the town for many years and was considered a good friend to the poor. A relative of Daniel's was Nathaniel Chandler, a councillor and Mayor of the town for three years, and whose portrait hangs in the council chamber. A lane ran from the end of the court into Mill Street, and was known as Carrs Lane in 1842, but prior to this, in the sixteenth century, it was known as Waites Lane. In Old English, *waite* meant a lookout. A house built in the Victorian period closes this end of the court.

## Old Baptist Chapel Court

Quite probably a unique area, in that it houses one the oldest surviving Baptist chapels in the country. When this building was being renovated in the early 1970s, the original water

baptismal trough was found beneath the floor. There is a gallery around the main chapel area, and scratched on the walls are the names of those Baptists who became bored with the preacher during the long and painful sermons. At the top of the court is the old Baptist burial ground, where the local members were buried. Here lies one John Shakespeare Hart, reputedly a descendant of the Bard of Avon. He was a chair maker living in Barton Street in the nineteenth century.

## Turners Court

Mr Turner was a stocking weaver who lived here, and was reputedly a thrifty man, as he saved his money and bought a horse and cart and became a carrier, plying his trade between Tewkesbury, Cheltenham and Gloucester. His other claim to fame was that he had been wounded while serving in the Royal Navy, and received a pension of six pence per day! In 1842, this was known as Freemans Court, not to be confused with a court of the same name in Barton Street.

## CHURCH STREET

### Smiths Court

Now an alley that leads from Church Street through to St Marys Lane, this was also called Insalls Court. Mr Insall was a cordwainer, (boot and shoe maker), in the nineteenth century. This court has a very narrow entrance that widens out to meet the rear of No. 75 Church Street. The alley houses one of the only two hand water pumps in the town.

### Laights Court

The nameplate from this court has not been seen for some years, but it still carries this family name. Edward Laight lived here in the mid–1800s, and was a teacher. He ran a school, or at least a series of classes, for some years, in the top floor room of Cross House.

### Post Office Lane

So called because the post office was sited here until about 1965. The lane was called Bank Lane in 1868, and after this, in 1880, was known as Parsons Lane. It provided access to the old tan yards, and led through to Tolsey Lane. The building on the front of Church Street was a bank until the 1920s.

## Tolsey Lane

The name comes from the fact that the Tolsey or town hall, was sited near the lane. The last tolsey was removed to widen the road near The Cross in 1789, and was the third one on that site. The lane leads down to the River Avon and was once the site of the builders yard for Thomas Collins. Here there were two small courts: Catherines and Nailors. The latter comprised a few small cottages, fitted up by Mr Barnes, a local ironmonger, with a small workshop in the kitchen, for the purpose of nail making.

## Priors Alley

Another family name, coming from a local councillor and mayor of the town by the name of Prior. This alley is now much shorter than it originally was, due to the re-development of this area with residential building.

## HIGH STREET

## Wilkes Alley

This is to be found part way up the High Street and takes its name from a Mr Wilkes who had a tinsmiths business on the frontage. The alley used to run down to the Mill Avon, but in around 1965, a new housing development took place and the alley was diverted. Here

The north side of Church Street, with the entrance to Laights Court.

there were several cottages, occupied until the demolition, having just one cold-water tap, and a shared toilet facility. The cholera epidemic of 1831 began here, killing several of those living in the alley.

## Smiths Lane

A road in reality, this area probably got its name from the fact that there was a smith's workshop directly opposite the pub on the left-hand side of the frontage. At the bottom of the lane there were two small courts: Sweets and Birds, which were both occupied until about 1940. They both had five or six cottages, with a shared washhouse and toilet facility in the yard. This was also the site of the Hen and Chickens public house.

## Machine Court

Although now a court, this was once an alley going from the High Street down to the Mill Avon, and is recorded as such in 1842. The name is likely to be derived from the fact that most of the cottages in the alleys hired stocking knitting machines for quite a long period in the 1800s. It was possible to rent a cottage and a machine from the owner, for the sum of 2s per week.

## Cares Alley

William Cares had his butchers shop here, at the top of the alley. It has also been recorded as Kears Alley, but I believe that this was just an error of transposition. The passage has been closed off as an alley for many years.

## Brays Court

This was another alley that led down to the river, but was closed off at some time. A stonemason named Bray lived here, and was responsible for building the cottages in the alley. He hired a man called John Brimmell, who had dual skills, being not only a builder, but also a rope maker. He had an area in Rope Walk, which he used for laying out his ropes.

## Clarkes Alley

The Misses Clarke lived here in the nineteenth century, and ran a small school for young ladies, which was perhaps something like a Dames School. The alley runs down to the river and has a slightly different feature, in that the paved floor has raised brickwork on the slope down to the river. This would give purchase to the housewife going to get her water from

*Opposite:* Clarkes Alley, High Street, with its raised brickwork to facilitate climbing the slope, especially in inclement weather.

the river, and for the delivery of goods from the barges into the High Street, by horses. The alley was also called Clerks Alley in 1820, (which may be another mis-spelling), Dobbins Alley in 1842, after the gentleman who owned Dobbins Row in Oldbury Road, and Wilkinsons Alley in 1870.

## Hammerton Court

George Hammerton lived here in the middle of the nineteenth century. He was called a bargeman in the census returns, but in reality he was a barge owner. He ran the Market Boat from Tewkesbury to Gloucester for two days each week. The arrival of the railway in 1840 however, began to take trade off the river and affected Hammerton and others in the town.

## Lock Court

Unlike most of the other alleys, this is not a family name. The alley used to pass from the High Street down to the river, and in the alley was a cottage allocated to the lock keeper. Before the lock keeper's cottage on the side of the river was built, the lock keeper would be called to operate the lock from his cottage in the alley. He would probably have a small boat or a punt moored on the river, and would row across to the lock to undertake the task.

## Manns Court

William Mann was recorded as a waterman in the census returns, but in reality was a barge owner and a coal merchant, with the two professions going hand in hand. He is reputed to have owned all the property in the alley. He too, would have suffered, in business terms, from the coming of the railway, as it was considered cheaper and faster.

## Stephens Alley

The Stephens were a comparatively prosperous family, owning most of the property in this alley. There were a number of small cottages here, most of which would be used by the occupants to make stockings to sell to the Stephens family. A little further up the alley on the right hand side, is a row of houses called Dovers Cottages. One of the family of Stephens was town lamplighter for over thirty years, when the streets were lit by oil and wick. He went by the nickname of 'Lampy Loo Stephens'.

## Well Alley

This is in an area reputed to be the site of the town's early water supply. John Rogers, writing in around 1900, expresses the view that this was where the first town well was situated, and was where the Romans would have settled in Tewkesbury. This, of course, was born out when the old Sabrina Cinema site was excavated and Roman remains and artefacts were discovered. He also stated that there was a natural spring running beneath the cellar of one of the houses at the Oldbury Road end of the alley.

## Summers Court

This was always a court and was named after Mary Summers, a lady who owned a Lodging House here in the nineteenth century. There were four timber-framed cottages in the alley. The lady catered for tramps and travellers, but after many reports to the authorities, the police closed down this 'low lodging house'.

## Eagles Alley

George Eagles was a butcher who ran his business from the front of the High Street in around 1836. There is also a record of this being known as Hodges Alley in 1750. This area was the subject of an official inquiry, when a national company wished to divert the alley in order to build a small supermarket. After the company won the appeal, the alley was diverted, and the shop was built. Its success was short lived, however, as it closed down after only a short time in business. At the time of Mr Eagle's residence, there were several families living here, one of which was called Moss. The father was a stocking maker and a cycle repairer, while one son became a travelling grinder and chimney sweep!

## Warders Alley

The alley as it is today would not be recognisable as that of the nineteenth century. The cottages have gone and we just have a passageway between High Street and Oldbury Road. Richard Warder was a cordwainer, or shoemaker, living here in the 1800s. The Cordwainers Guild was formed sometime in the fifteenth century, and was only wound up in around 1940 when the last four members of the guild met in the Wheatsheaf pub to close the guild. Some of the artefacts have been saved in the Museum while other documents are kept in the Records Office in Gloucester.

## Malverns Alley

There is no indication of the name of the alley, but the alternative name of Haywards Alley will identify the location as being between the hardware shop and what is now a motor spares shop. The passage runs through to Oldbury Road and would have had several two and three storied cottages. These were latterly used as workshops for the Hayward, but only one now remains, just behind the main shop building.

## Old Post Office Alley

This was logically named from the business, which was conducted on the High Street frontage. This alley housed a substantial number of stocking-frame workers, while at the

*Left:* Walls Court, off the High Street. This view from around 1930, looks toward the High Street, with the Nottingham Arms on the right hand side.

*Opposite:* Barton Street. There is no traffic about so the streets are quite safe. The errand boy is out doing his deliveries and it is still acceptable for the children to play outside.

Oldbury Road end of the alley there was a stocking shop owned by Mr Key. He also hired out the stocking frames. The original post office building was demolished in around 1870, and a Mr Fluck, who was also involved in the building of a mill for Mr Rice on the Ham, built the existing building.

## Walls Court

This is no longer a court, but a through way to Oldbury Road, and named after Mr Wall, a tailor who owned the shop on the High Street. Until some fifty years ago, a row of toilets, shared by the residents of the alley, stood at the top of what was then a court. These were demolished in around 1940, giving access to Oldbury Road. The old Bakery, which was owned by Cecil Crouch, a baker with two shops in the town, still stands and is now a highly priced dwelling house.

## Merretts Yard

Until the 1940s, this was an area having eight or nine cottages in it. There is no record of its old name, but Mr Merrett kept a butchers shop on the High Street, which is now a greengrocers, and used the rear entrance to get to the yard where he lived.

## BARTON STREET

### Fryzers Court

The court carries the name of the family of Fryzers, and the court originally had four cottages that were built by the father, Samuel Fryzer. He was a brick manufacturer, with his works at The Mythe. Here there were several brick makers, all taking the clay from the banks of the Severn. The entrance to the court is dark and gloomy, but it opens up into a large and pleasant garden area. The son of Samuel Fryzer lived here and practiced as a solicitor.

### Alexander Court

This was originally known as Crooked Alley, because there is five bends in it. The alley was the main through road to Oldbury Road until Nelsons Alley was widened to become Nelson Street. The Oldbury Road end of the alley is still visible as a small entrance in the corner of Nelson Street and Oldbury Road.

Barton Street and Nelson Street. The Nelson Inn is closed and ready for demolition. To the left of the building would have been Huntleys Court.

## Charlewood Alley

Now just a passageway through from Barton Street to East Street, this was once a populated area. The name comes from the proprietor of a tailors and drapers shop, who lived in the front house. Prior to this name, it was known as Harewoods Alley, which was another family name.

## Davis Alley

Mr Davis had a shop on the right hand side of the front, and was a purveyor of bacon and other foodstuffs – probably what we would call a pork butcher. He had the nickname of 'Chitterlings George', because of the quality of his produce! The alley goes through from Barton Street to East Street.

## Hayes Court

In the middle of the nineteenth century, George Hayes was in business as a cabinet maker, with a shop on the front. In 1900, this was an alley going through to East Street, but is now closed off and is just an access to the house on the front. The entrance is dark and narrow, and typical of the Victorian style.

## Potters Court

Standing close to the Watson Hall, the front building has recently been restored. The alley is at the eastern side of the building and goes through to Saffron Walk and Swilgate Road. In the early part of the nineteenth century, the Potters were a family of Weavers, with Mr Potter seeing off three wives in his eighty-seven years. His son carried on living here and became a plumber.

## Yarnalls Alley

William and Richard Yarnall had a chair making business here through the mid-1800s. The entrance to the alley shows the original timbers, standing on raised blocks to prevent decay. Richard Yarnall was a supporter of the French Revolution, and was known locally as Jacobite Yarnall.

## Fish Alley

This alley did in fact have two names: Fish Alley East and Fish Alley West, the latter being the entrance from Barton Street. On the left hand side were four cottages, while there was only one on the right. This gave an open space for a drying area. Part way down the alley was an archway leading to the lower part of the alley.

## Hughes Alley

Joe Hughes had a shop on the front selling milk butter and dairy products. The alley goes from Barton Street down to Swilgate Road. Mr Hughes kept his cows on pasture at Perry Hill, and in his field was the large elm tree known as Wesley's Elm, for it was here that John Wesley preached when he visited the town. Myrtle Court led off this alley to the left hand side. At the bottom were workshops used at one time for the making of sack bags, probably for the Workhouse, and the alley was known by this name for some time. Opposite the Swilgate Brook end of the alley, stood a small building on the side of Swilgate Brook. This was known as 'Tommy Craddocks Duckhouse', and was in use as a wash house for residents, using the water from the brook. It was taken down sometime in the 1960s.

## Comptons Alley

The Comptons were a family in business at the house on the eastern side of the entrance, manufacturing and selling furniture. This alley also goes down to Swilgate Road, and would have had properties on both sides. At the bottom of the alley, the local council built three privies for the use of the residents; their stated aim in the 1930s was to provide one toilet for every twenty persons!

Church Street, with Savings Bank alley, Ancills Court and Lilleys Alley.

## Chapel Court

This was the entrance to an old posting house called The Star and Garter, the entrance leading to stables at the rear. Just inside the entrance, high on the right-hand wall, it is possible to see the old balustrade, built into the wall. The Baptist chapel was built at the rear in 1801, hence the name. Recently however, a new chapel has been built and the old one demolished.

## Masons Court

This court is at the end of Barton Street, close to The Cross. In the middle of the nineteenth century, Mr Mason lived here and owned all the property in the court. He was a bachelor, and when he died he left all his property to his housekeeper, who then married the tailor living on the frontage.

## Ancills Court

This was an alley named after John Ancill, but is now closed off. It provides the entrance to the Berkeley Arms, one of the oldest pubs in the town, and originally passed through to the Swilgate Road. Behind the pub is an early half-timbered medieval hall, which is now renovated and in use as a dwelling.

## Lilleys Alley

This is one of the earliest alleys in the town and one of the most beautiful. In about 1805, a lady called Mary Lilley had a china shop on the front of Church Street, which she rented from Hosier called 'Corkleg Packer'! In one the sixteenth century timber framed cottages, clay pipes were made and hung out to dry on the racks along the walls.

## CHANCE STREET

Chance Street indicates the limit of the towns development until the Enclosure Act released land for building, *c.* 1810. The piece of land immediately to the east of Chance Street was called The Pound.

## North East Terrace

Originally built in about 1830, this was a lace-making factory for many years. The owner also built a number of cottages in a court next to the Congregational church in Barton Street, for his workers. The business eventually ran out of steam, and despite further attempts to make stockings, it closed. Now these are sought after dwellings. They are known locally as Chimney Pot Row, and a glance at the roofline will explain why.

## Union Place

This is located in Chance Street and was originally part of Speculation Place. The whole of this area was developed after the Enclosure Act of 1808, and gave the town the opportunity of building further away from the three main streets. This alley leads down to The Folly, where there are some nice open areas and detached houses.

## Trinity Walk

A through walk from Oldbury Road to Chance Street, built when the Trinity School was developed. There is also a small block of houses called Trinity Place here. The school closed in the mid-1970s and it is now the Masonic Hall.

## Rope Walk

Leading off Chance Street, Rope Walk is part of the development that took place after the Enclosure Act, which opened up all that area from Oldbury Road, almost through to Ashchurch Road. This was the area used by the rope makers to lay out their ropes and set up their wheels, on each side of the original Rope Lane. When the development took place, this right was lost.

*Above:* Lilleys Alley, Church Street.

*Left:* Lilleys Alley from Church Street.

*Opposite:* Lilleys Alley leading onto Church Street. The timber-framed building on the right is probably from the sixteenth century and is still in good repair. The hand water pump served the occupants of the alley until piped water became available.

## OLDBURY ROAD

### Old Hospital Lane

Just off Oldbury Road to the north end, stands Tracy Row. This small row of houses backs onto a short stretch of road, Old Hospital Lane. The name is taken from the fact that it was here that the first Rural Hospital was set up by Dr Devereux, a local surgeon. The money was raised by public subscription, and provided a single room, with one bed, one bath and one nurse! It led, however, to the establishment of a true hospital, further along Oldbury Road, which is now converted for use as sheltered accommodation for elderly people.

### Gravel Walk

This is an area developed in about 1833, and is so called because it was built in an area of gravel deposits. The passageway goes from Oldbury Road to Cotteswold Road, and has a wide variety of terraced, detached and semi-detached houses. On the south side of the walk there is a row of four cottages, built shortly afterwards, by a developer by the name of Mr Green, and so are called, yes, Green's Buildings!

These are the alleys and courts that remain after the demolition which took place in 1965. There were many properties in this area of the town that were not worth saving, but by far the greater number should have been saved for the town. Sadly, the many timber-framed cottages and all the carved timbers were thrown on the fires at the rear of the High Street, which seemed to burn for weeks.

CHAPTER TWELVE

# Tewkesbury Tales

Local people have, in the main, passed the following stories to me during talks to local groups, and they have also come from research sources.

## Nellie Jones Shop

This was located at the upper end of the High Street, close to Double Alley. The woman's name was Helen Jones, but everyone knew her as Nellie, and she was a general retailer, selling sweets, fruit and vegtables' and other foodstuffs. Locals will tell that she had the first ice-cream making machine in the town, and the children could, if they were prepared to, turn the handle on the machine to crush the ice for fifteen minutes, and receive a free ice cream for their hard work. She had an ongoing battle with the local constabulary, because she placed her boxes of goods on the pavement outside the shop, pretty much as what happens today. The local constable, probably as a result of a complaint, wanted these boxes removed. Nellie refused and after some wrangling, when the police threatened to take legal action, she informed them that as the goods were in line with the two steps, which went up from the pavement to the shop, and were her property, that they could not touch her. The matter was never heard of again, and is a victory for common sense.

## Doddo Café

This was the large timber-framed property, situated close to the previous shop, and was for many years the place where local people met, had tea or coffee, and gossiped.
Inside was a large doorway, studded in the medieval style, and which had reputedly come from the Abbey, possibly at the dissolution. This was the general view in the town.

However, while talking to the head of an old established building firm, I was informed that this doorway was in fact put together by them using ancient timbers, and installed in the café, probably some time in the early part of the twentieth century! I think I like the original myth better!

## Mary Atwoods Shop

Another shop that most local people will remember was this one in Barton Street. The inside of the shop had no kind of order; with the shelves packed with everything a shop could sell. Tins of beans rubbed shoulders with jars of jam; sweets and shoe polish would lie next to each other, together with bacon and ham. It was the original 'Open All Hours' shop, and Mary herself was always obliging and friendly. She was a short plump lady who never married, but who always seemed happy. She had help from a lady called Miss Quarrell, who was a schoolteacher and who helped in the shop in her spare time.

## Ghosts

Being such an ancient town and having such royal associations, the town has its share of ghost stories, with tunnels under the streets, leading to and from the abbey, ghostly figures of monks in hooded cloaks and so on. Recently, while talking to the proprietor of the Bistro at the crescent in Church Street, I was told of one that was new to me. Inside the bistro is a room at the rear, used as part of the dining area, with a stairway, beside which was placed a chair. On one occasion, the owner saw an elderly lady sitting there and thought it was a customer. After serving someone in the other room, she came back to find the lady had gone. However, upon asking the staff and looking around, no trace could be found of this special visitor.

## Characters

The town has always seemed to have its share of 'characters'. John Moore in his book, *Portrait of Elmbury*, talks of Pistol, Bardolph and Nym – three of the roguish characters of whom Shakespeare wrote, and whom he thought were reflected in three of the people he had met in the town. These were identifiable of course, and were known locally. They were quietly visible in and around the town and were always polite, saying 'yes sir' or 'your worship', whenever they spoke. My first encounter with them, was on a quiet Sunday afternoon, while listening to the radio, (before television), when there was a knock on the door, and Mr Underwood and Mr Drinkwater politely asked if we would be interested in buying a quantity of mushrooms or a rabbit! Uncertain as to the origin, we declined the offer, after which they thanked us and went to the next house. Mr Drinkwater could have made a good living in the building trade, as he was an excellent bricklayer, according to one local builder. It is stated that in order to try and keep him out of trouble, he was commissioned to build the curved wall that went around the front of the Trinity Church.

They did, of course, have their descendants, with one being an ex soldier who had been in North Africa, and the other who I believe was a cousin, was to follow in the illustrious footsteps of the original three. Latterly, Jack could usually be found sitting on the bench in front of the Town Hall wearing an army greatcoat and white plimsoll shoes, always clean and white, waiting for the supermarket to open for his supply of alcohol. He washed and shaved every day at the public toilets, which were situated in Sun Street at the time.

On one occasion, he and Aubrey were living in an old Rover car, kept on the cricket field for pulling the large roller. Feeling the need for refreshment, Jack sent his partner to the shop in Abbots Road, Priors Park, which was also an Off Licence, with instructions to bring something to drink. Later Aubrey returned with a bottle of sherry, upon which he was berated and told to go back and obtain something a little stronger. By the time he reached the shop of course, the local bobby was waiting and both had a short rest at Gloucester!

Another character, who was part of a local building firm, was walking along East Street one day, when a lady dashed out of her house crying. She asked the gentleman to come and have a look at her husband. They went upstairs and the husband was lying on the bed. 'I'm sorry my dear, but I'm afraid he be djud',(dead), he said, and without more ado, he took a tape from his pocket and measured him up for coffin, with a final word, that 'he must go out the window as the stairs be too narrow'.

## Bargus' Fish and Chip Shop

Reputed to have sold the nicest fish and chips in the town, Bargus' was situated in Barton Street, in the same shop as the present chippy. They were there for many years, both before and after the Second World War. You could buy standard fish and chips, or a packet of fish bits, and even four scallops for a penny! After the war they moved to Cheltenham and ran the same business in Regent Street. In the early 1950s, this was Wales Fish Shop and they also had the shop next door to the west, using it as a Restaurant.

Another shop selling the same products was in Trinity Street, in the wooden building which became a boot and shoe repair shop. During the war a family called Hewitt, no relation to Harry Hewitt and his brother, ran it for some years.

Tustin's 'chippy' was in Oldbury Road, just opposite Gravel Walk, later run by Mr Storey, before he took over the same business in Quay Street.

## Watson Hall

This building has a long history of entertainment of all kinds, from orchestral concerts when it was a philharmonic hall to old time music hall, and even a period when wrestling was staged there in an effort to make it pay it's way.

However, the Saturday night dances will be in most people's memory. Here the local bands played: Jack Wilkins, Don Wilkes, supplemented by casual players like Ted Bufton, and occasional singers, such as Derek Graham. The floor, which was full of knots, would be liberally sprinkled with talcum powder before the dance to ensure a slippery surface! At the rear of the hall were two rows of fixed seats, and the toilets were at each side of the entrance. There was no bar, of course, but it was only a short step to the Nelson.

After closing time, there would be an influx of part-time dancers, some better than others. Two small gentlemen, Tommy Wilkins and his friend, slightly the worse for wear, but extremely polite, would dance together for the last hour, which is a sight not seen since the hall was renovated in 1960.

There were also dances held at Ashchurch Camp. They were very popular affairs with buses bringing in dancers from all the surrounding villages. There was always a band, mostly Al Kessel from Cheltenham, but others too, with a charge I think of two shillings in the early 1950s.

## The Sabrina

The Sabrina was the local theatre of dreams, with a change of programme twice each week. It had a balcony, with front and rear seating. At the very back, on each side of the central stairway, were two separate seats, usually occupied by two couples, who were oblivious to the film and the other filmgoers! On the upper floor was a restaurant that catered for parties and weddings. When a popular film was on, the steps to the rear balcony would be used as seats.

## Wheatsheaf

A beautiful timber framed building that almost looks too top-heavy, mid-way along the High Street, with oak panelled walls and a passageway on the left hand side, leading to the rear. We are fortunate that it survived in such good condition for so long, especially considering the landlord who, upon smelling gas one night, came downstairs and lit a match to look for the leak! It does not only happen in comics – this really took place. Fortunately no one was hurt badly but it was a salutary lesson nonetheless.

## Camping

For many years Tewkesbury had a regular influx of visitors, especially from Birmingham, who arrived at the start of the annual Midlands two weeks holiday to set up camp. The campsite was situated at the King George playing fields, on the area now occupied by the Bowling and Rugby Clubs. On other school holidays, the fathers would go back to work in Brum on the Sunday night and return at the weekend to pick up the family. There was lots of football, and fishing in Swilgate Brook and sometimes there would be a small fairground on the Pageant Meadow or up the Mythe Road at the Breaking Stone Meadow, to take care of the evenings. The other site was at the Twyning meadows, alongside the river.

## Cricket Club

Tewkesbury Cricket Club was formed before 1840, and is one of the oldest clubs in the county. The odd thing is that when it was formed, there was no ground to play on and the first recorded matches, four in one season, were all played at Bushley, probably on what was the Common. The club played on the Ham, on Mitton Leys, on the orchard that is now Oldfield Estate, and on the field opposite Safeway over several years until the Swilgate field was let to them by a local farmer, B.T. Moore. They have played there since 1869.

In 1896, Tewkesbury played Malvern on Whit Monday, and 1,000 spectators watched the match. In this year there were five members of the Healing family playing for the club.

On 24 August 1878, a cricket match took place between six of the Tewkesbury Club using broomsticks, and twelve juniors selected from local clubs, using bats. The age and strength of the six proved too much for the juniors, with some of the balls being driven a great distance. The scorecard disappeared with the juniors and was not seen again!

## Sir Raymond Priestlay

A story that Sir Raymond told of his youth and the Methodist church, was passed to me a few years ago. The minister at the church was endeavouring to raise funds for the church and asked for donations from the congregation. An elderly gentleman sitting in the balcony called out 'five shillings'. At that moment a piece of plaster fell from the ceiling and struck him on the head. 'Ten shillings', he cried, at which the minister raised his eyes to the heavens and called 'hit him again Lord, hit him again'!

## Oldfield

At an auction held on 21 July 1954, the land at Oldfield, which was at that time, mostly orchard, plus 5.75 acres off the Ashchurch Road, were sold for £4,100, at the Swan Hotel. What a price today!

## Scavenger

Before proper sanitation reached the town, the population used 'night soil privies'. These were shared facilities, of which there were one or two in the alley, mostly single seaters. The toilet consisted of a wooden seat with a hole, and underneath was a bucket part filled with soil or ashes. These would have a square brick shelter and a door and would be situated at one end of the alley. At night the soil would be taken out and dumped, either at the and of the alley or in the street. The scavenger, a man hired by the Town Council, would collect the waste on his cart, between the hours of midnight and five in the morning. His contract required that he must not use the cart for any other purpose! One cannot imagine what! The cart was then driven out of town, mostly to Walton Cardiff, and dumped in a field!

These essential edifices at the bottom of the garden, or up the alley, have brought new and interesting words into the language: 'being caught with one's trousers down', having its origin behind the foot-wedged door. 'Bum fodder' led to our present usage of 'bumph' for lots of paperwork.

Toilet paper of course developed from the need for a more luxurious material than the local newspaper, hung by it's corner on a string behind the door.

In shared facilities such as these, one had to be able to whistle or sing to prevent intrusions, especially if these were double-seaters!

## Working Days

Work in the early part of the 1900s was long and hard with very little pay. One lady, aged ninety, told me of her early years at work.

Ginny Gibbard, (née Walker), was put into service at the age of thirteen, with a farmer at Upton-on-Severn. She lived in, did the cleaning, washing and ironing, in something like a fourteen-hour day. She had one half day per week as time off, but had to be back at work the same evening. She received bed and board, and a payment of 2s 6d per week, most of which went to her family. After several weeks of this job, she decided she had had enough, and left the farm and walked back to her home in Bank Alley. The very next morning her mother walked her back to the farm at Upton, to resume her position! Who of us would take that kind of punishment today?

## Sgt F.C. Reade

On 18 February 1922, Drill Sgt Reade was charged by the police with having stolen nine pairs of army trousers and nine pairs of army boots, which were the property of the Fifth Batt, the Gloucestershire Regiment. The police stated that the prisoner had a very good war record and had been helpful in their enquiries. He was unemployed and had no home. The court found him guilty and sentenced him to one month in gaol, without hard labour. This sentence meant that he was not deprived of his army pension of 10s per week. There is no record of him living in the town, or of any relatives. Where did he go?

## 1809

The *Gloucestershire Notes and Queries* records unusual items, beginning in 1808. A report in Vol 1 refers to the Tewkesbury Corporation celebrating the 50th anniversary of the accession of George III to the throne:

> At the celebration of the Jubilee, 1809, the Corporation of Tewkesbury, with the Volunteer Cavalry, attended divine service. Four oxen, with a due share of potatoes and beer, were distributed among upwards of 3,000 people. A Ball was held at The Cross Keys in the evening, and was attended by a large and fashionable company.
>
> A local medal was presented by a gentleman of the first respectability, who holds a high official situation in the Borough, to the inhabitants of Tewkesbury and neighbouring families. Who was this gentleman and to where did the medal go?

## Piffs Elm 1844

Moore and Weaver sold the celebrated large and lofty elm, called Piffs Elm, which stood on the edge of the Turnpike Road, immediately in front of The Swan, or Piffs Elm, at auction, for the sum of £13, on 20 December 1844.

This tree was claimed by the Dean and Chapter of Westminster, as Lords of Elmstone Hardwicke. The tree was in ruins, but still magnificent and Mr Crook of Hasfield was the purchaser. It produced 500ft of perfectly sound timber. The planks were sought after by neighbourhood gentry to make tables and the like. Numerous snuffboxes were made by Mr Crook and disposed of as presents to his friends.

## Byelaws 1851

In a byelaw passed in 1851, relating to Lodging Houses, it was required that:

A water closet or privy shall be provided for every lodging house having a yard or other facilities for the erection the reof and where such facilities do not exist or where the closet or privy is used in common by the lodgers of two or more houses, the privy or closet must be provided in some place, convenient to the satisfaction of the Inspector, and for every twenty lodgers to be accommodated, a separate closet or privy shall be provided.

## Lodging House Survey

In February 1865, a survey of the lodging houses in the town took place for the local board of health. One run by James Hawkins in St Marys Lane was found to be 'filthy dirty, but with clean bedding'. Elizabeth Rickett's house was 'very filthy, with scarcely a pane of glass whole'. That must have been at the bottom of the league table. The owners were given five days to clean and whitewash their property.

## Complaint

In a report to the board of health, a complaint had been received of a nuisance on the premises of B. Webb of Barton Street, arising from the boiling of horseflesh at the property; 'It was ordered that proper steps be taken to compel the cessation'.

## Golf Club

In 1892 a golf club was formed at Shutonger Common. This was a nine hole course, built, as many are in Gloucestershire, on common land. The project was short lived, however, as the onset of the First World War seemed to put an end to the club.

## Sun Street

Before the redevelopment of the High Street, Sun Street was almost opposite the Anchor Hotel. Here, a row of small shops stood opposite the Tewkesbury Car Mart. There was a hairdresser and a cobbler in this row, and Preston the bespoke taylor had the premises on the High Street corner. A story told to me by a lady concerned the cobbler, who was her grandfather. He lived in Upton-on-Severn, and when the weather was good, he would swim from Upton to Tewkesbury to get to his shop! It is a good story, but I don't know if it is just a lot of cobblers!

# Afterword

## Tewkesbury Wills

On the database at Tewkesbury Library, there are details of Tewkesbury wills, dating from the fifteenth century. These were researched by Cameron Talbot and Bill Rennison of the Tewkesbury Historical Society. A great deal of information is contained within these documents, but I was struck by the number of wills, which carried the names of the alleys and courts recorded in the town. The following list gives just a few of the names from those wills that have become familiar in my research.

| 1605 | Martha Kedward | Widow |
|------|----------------|-------|
| 1616 | Martha Jeynes | Occupation unknown |
| 1621 | John Jeynes | Occupation unknown |
| 1647 | Thomas Boulter | Mason |
| 1649 | Thomas Mansell | Glazier |
| 1662 | William Dobbins | Maltster |
| 1675 | Samuel Millard | Tailor |
| 1682 | Nathanial Jeynes | Joiner |
| 1688 | Henry Dobbins | Gent. |
| 1689 | Nathanial Jeynes | Occupation unknown |
| 1699 | Mandlin Huntley | Widow |
| 1788 | John Spilsbury | Surgeon/Apothecary |

The alleys which have carried these names do not necessarily refer directly to people listed above, although John Spilsbury does apply. They are an indication of the antiquity of these families. They and others recur throughout several centuries of the town's history.

# Conclusion

THE PRECEDING CHAPTERS GIVE a brief insight into the development of the town since the seventeenth century, when the alleys began to grow. The astounding fact is that there have been so many changes over a relatively short time, in such a limited area of the town, with the majority of these alleys being in the three main streets.

Several times over the past years, I thought I had come to the end of my task, only to receive a phone call or an email, asking if I had heard of yet another alley! Punch Bowl Alley is an example, where I was set on yet another chase after a location and a description. So I expect that out there, there are still others to find, but this will be for someone else to search.

I hope that this small work will have some interest, not only for all those who live in Tewkesbury, but also for the many visitors who wish to know a little more about this superb town.

# Index

# Other local titles published by Tempus

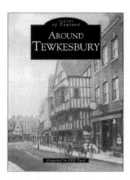

## Around Tewkesbury
CLIFF BURD

In this pictorial record the reader is taken on a tour of the town, looking at how it has progressed and developed throughout the decades of the twentieth century. It will provide older residents of the area with a nostalgic look at the recent past and bring to newcomers an opportunity to look at how things used to be.

0 7524 2273 1

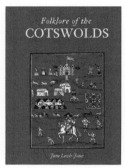

## Folklore of the Cotswolds
JUNE LEWIS-JONES

This detailed book explores the heritage of folklore that has always been so prevalent throughout the Cotswolds. Cures and remedies, recipes, traditions, dance and song, are explored and legends born of the landscape, such as the Devil's Chimney and the Rollright Stones, and lesser-known Cotswold stories like the secret marriage at Snowshill Manor are highlighted here.

0 7524 2930 2

## The Flying Machine in Gloucestershire
DEREK N. JAMES

Gloucestershire has been home to an active aviation industry since the dawn of manned powered flight. From the early balloon flights to Britain's first jet aeroplane this book tells the story of Gloucestershire's contribution to flight in all its forms.

0 7524 3113 7

## Gloucester RFC From Pilkington to Powergen
IAN RANDALL

This remarkable book follows the fortunes of Gloucester from the depths of despair following the Pilkington final against Northampton to the glorious aftermath of the Powergen win in 2003 – which confirmed the club's position as the finest in the land.

0 7524 3120 X

If you are interested in purchasing other books published by Tempus, or in case you have difficulty finding any Tempus books in your local bookshop, you can also place orders directly through our website

**www.tempus-publishing.com**

or from    **BOOKPOST**, Freepost, PO Box 29, Douglas, Isle of Man, IM99 1BQ
tel  01624 836000    email  bookshop@enterprise.net